THE COUNTY OF SALOP STEAM ENGINE SOCIETY
Glorious Years

Editor & Society Archivist:
Mike Llewellyn

Design & Production:
Steve Whitefoot

Proof Readers:
Joan & Jim Cook and Hedd Jones

Published by:
The County of Salop Steam Engine Society Ltd
PO Box 4706, Shrewsbury, Shropshire SY5 0WT
www.shrewsburysteamrally.co.uk

Cover Photos:
The class of 61 - A line up of engines that
attended the first rally in 1961 and the
50th Anniversary Rally in 2011.

From left to right:-

Fowler 'Cynorthwywr'
    (Works No.15787 - Reg. EP 2398)

Ruston & Hornsby 'Princess Anne'
    (Works No.52766 - Reg. AW 4996)

Ransomes Sims & Jefferies
    named 'Salopian' in 1961, now 'Lady Diana'
    (Works No.15609 - Reg. CJ 4220)

Ransomes Sims & Jefferies 'Jesse'
    (Works No.27524 - Reg. E 5123)

Marshall Tractor (roller in 61)
    (Works No.65650 - Reg BE 2227)

Aveling & Porter Roller 'Lady Hesketh'
    (Works No.9264 - Reg. EJ 966)

Fowler Showman's 'Supremacy'
    (Works No.15375 - Reg. UUP 526)

Front Cover: Malcolm Ranieri
Back Cover: Steve Whitefoot

This book is dedicated to the late Dennis Smith,
our founder, and all former members of the County
of Salop Steam Engine Society.

Acknowledgments

We would like to take this opportunity to thank the
photographers and photograph collection owners
for making contact and giving permission for us
to include their photographs in this book. Please
see the footnote to the individual photographs for
acknowledgement.

However we must give a very special mention to
Barry Finch, Bob Bailey, Harry Turner, Hedd Jones,
Malcolm Ranieri and Tony Thomas for their fantastic
support and help.

The images in the book have been selected on a fine
balance between photographic quality and historic
interest, and with over 350 engines having attended
our rallies over the last 50 years, it is physically
impossible to include a picture of them all and for this
we apologise in advance for any omissions.

Foreword

It was on my 20th birthday that the now famous challenge, by the late Arthur Napper of Appleford, to race his engine against one owned by a fellow farmer took place.

I had just completed my National Service in the R.A.F. as a photographer and the pictures published in the Daily Mirror of this event gave me the desire to photograph every engine I could find so that one day I would have a picture of every one in existence. It soon became apparent that this would never happen as more and more engines were found and beautifully restored when the rallies started to take place and their popularity spread throughout the country.

Fortunately many other people were taking pictures and many books were being published. However it did not seem possible back in the 1950's and 60's that the movement would develop the way that it has and to present such a wonderful selection of engines at the 50th Anniversary Rally of the County of Salop Steam Engine Society was a terrific achievement for the organising committee.

I sincerely hope that this publication will give a great deal of pleasure and interest to future generations and that the rally organisers, not only in Shropshire but nationwide, will continue to provide the occasions for many more people to see and admire the engines such as those depicted in this book.

I wish them all every success in the years to come.

Barry J. Finch

The very first Grand Parade in 1961, an idea which came from Dennis Smith. On the left is the Fowler 'Queen Mary' followed by a Clayton, both owned by Mike Salmon who, due to his Ring Steward duties, can be seen taking the opportunity to have a closer inspection of his engine. On the right is Bishop's Fowler 'Supremacy' followed by their Garrett 'Countess'.

Photo: Barry J. Finch

Preface

I spent my childhood at Stapleton, a small village about half a mile off the A49 trunk road, 5 miles south of Shrewsbury. I remember the sight, sound and even the smell of the threshing boxes visiting the local farms. The threshing contractors in question were Wynns of Frodesley, who by this time had stopped using steam engines and were instead using Allis Chalmers Model U tractors, metal Marshall threshing boxes and a Jones wire baler. I used to go down to Manor Farm, where my school friend lived, and watch the tackle in operation.

About mid-day on the Saturday before the 1960 August Bank Holiday, I could hear a strange sound of something very odd coming down the lane and then just a few minutes later, not just one but two traction engines passed the end of our drive. Our neighbour and friend, Gordon Warren seemed to think they were on route from Plealey to attend the Church Stretton Carnival which was to be held on the Bank Holiday Monday. It was with great excitement that we went to Church Stretton and found a spot in the crowds to stand and we saw several traction engines pass by at the head of the Carnival procession, including the two we had seen just two days earlier. I remember the news that the next years Carnival had been cancelled, but also the fantastic news that in its place was to be a Traction Engine Rally on the Bank Holiday Monday.

The following year I was just as excited to hear the sound once again of engines coming down the lane from the direction of Plealey, but this time there were three of them, an Aveling Roller (Reg. EJ 966) and a Ransome (Reg. E 5123), both belonging to Vin Nash, and a Ransome (Reg. CJ 4220) owned by Geoff Lee, who I later met in 1971 through my work as a Telephone Engineer when he was a Night Operator.

We went to that first Church Stretton Rally in 1961, which was truly fantastic, and the following Saturday my brother and I cycled down to the A49 and waited to see the engines return. This sowed the seed of interest and started me going to the rally as a must-do thing which has now lasted for over 50 years.

Some years later I met Charlie Bowen who was a crew member of Don Pritchard's Fowler D2 roller and it wasn't long before I was regularly going to Montgomery with Charlie to help Don on the roller along with Harry Turner. For the next 20 years we did a lot of work on the Fowler and spent many happy hours at Montgomery becoming almost one of the family. It was a set of six working day pictures of local engines which Don had, that he kindly allowed me to make copies of, which formed the nucleus of my picture collection. It was also through Don, a former Threshing Contractor himself, that I met his good friend Mr Dick Tanner who had also been a Threshing Contractor and had previously owned the Fowler engines 'Cynorthwywr', 'Monty' and the Garrett Tractor which was later named 'Rob Roy'. Dick also gave me many pictures to add to my collection.

Over the years I've had the chance to purchase two engines - a Ruston roller that lived for many years in Dons yard and later a Ruston Portable belonging to the Tanners of Newtown, Powys. But for various reasons and much to my regret it never happened.

Many years after I joined the County of Salop Steam Engine Society, it was decided that we should have an archivist and I was to be the first choice. I had just taken early retirement from a career spanning 40 years with BT, so luckily I was able to start work on the task and spent a lot of time getting the project off the ground. I was very keen to see if I could find the Photographer and Author, Mr Barry J. Finch, as I knew he had been to our rally at Church Stretton in 1961, 62, 64 and 66 and then Bishop's Castle in 1970 and had taken many fine black and white pictures. So I made several phone calls and wrote one or two letters, even a request on the Traction Talk website, but to no avail. Then one day out of the blue I had a phone call and a gentleman's voice said 'I understand you've been after me". It was indeed, Mr Barry J. Finch himself and since that day we have had many conversations and become good friends. And it was with great pleasure that we met Barry and his wife at our 50th Anniversary Rally.

It rapidly became apparent that we had more than enough material for a photographic archive book of the last 50 years, but the major problem was how to choose about 200 prints from the vast archive - This book is the result of this work I hope you find it of interest.

Michael J Llewellyn
Society Archivist
The County of Salop Steam Engine Society

CHURCH STRETTON

Even though the origins of the Society go back as far as 1955, when engines owned by Dick Woolley and the Bishop brothers of Burley were entered in the first Church Stretton Carnival, the County of Salop Steam Engine Society was not actually formed until the 7th June 1961 at a meeting in the Bucks Head, Church Stretton.

Dennis Smith had the plans for the 1961 Church Stretton Carnival well underway, when suddenly like a bolt out of the blue, one Saturday morning in June; he was stopped in the street in Church Stretton and told that the Carnival was cancelled as there was a lack of interest and a big shortage of floats. Dennis thought that if that was the case, then the steam enthusiasts should go it alone and have a Traction Engine Rally. Without any further delay he went straight down the adjoining passage and into the printers, Mr Arty Williams and asked him whether he could print the programme and posters. He said that this he would do and as Dennis left Arty shouted after him, "What are you going to call it? It must have a name, you know". Dennis thought for a moment and then replied, "The County of Salop Steam Engine Society". And so we were born!

A meeting soon took place on 7th June, 1961 with Dennis as Chairman, who was also to be the Rally Organiser for the first rally, which was going to be held on Monday 7th August, but Dennis later resigned from being Chairman at a meeting held just after the rally on 30th August, so that he could focus on his role as Rally Organiser. And so Norman Owen took on the role of Chairman.

The 1966 Church Stretton Grand Parade (*from left to right*) Fowler 'Supremacy', Fowler 'Queen Mary', Burrell Scenic 'Winston Churchill' and Burrell 'Rajah'.
Photo: Harry Turner

Our Founder - Dennis Smith *(right)* at the 1957 Church Stretton Carnival on his Ruston, Proctor & Co. Traction Engine (Works No.52266 - Reg. CJ 4178) which he purchased in 1955. He's joined by Reg Wheeler *(left)* who was also an early driving force and owned a Burrell Gold Medal Tractor (Works No.3786 - Reg. PB 9610).

Photo: Susan Edge (Reg Wheeler's Daughter)

Foden Steam Tractor 'Cymru am Byth', translated means 'Wales for ever'. (Works No.13832 - Reg. HX 2197) Seen here in the 1958 Carnival, owned by W.A. Bishop & Sons of Burley, having just crossed the railway bridge in Sandford Avenue with the station yard visible in the background. The tractor is a cut down 6 ton wagon, now named 'The Dorset Wanderer'.

Photo: Ken Watkins

Sentinel S4 (Works No.9346 - Reg. CXB 783) at the 1958 Church Stretton Carnival and owned by Dick Woolley. It was still very much a working Tar Sprayer, going to Welshpool on almost a daily basis to collect tar from The Midland Tar Distiller's. The tank held 1,200 gallons of steam heated tar. The Waggon was driven by Ted Proctor, a true steam man, and his fireman Danny Jones from Knighton. They kept the Waggon in very fine condition indeed - just look at the gleaming tank.

Photo: Ken Watkins

Fowler D5 Road Locomotive 'Cynorthwywr' (Works No.15787 - Reg. EP 2398) seen here nearing the top of Sandford Avenue in the 1959 Carnival, owned and driven by R. Phillips of Leebotwood having recently been purchased from Mr Dick Tanner of Caersws near Newtown. Behind we see the Foden steam tractor 'Cymru am Byth' (Works No.13832 - Reg. HX 2197) owned by W.A. Bishop & Sons of Burley.

Photo: Mr & Mrs Crowther

The route of the Carnival procession was approximately three-quarters of a mile long and the engines can be seen here in 1958 coming down Burway Road and turning into Shrewsbury Road. Prizes were presented once the procession had reached the carnival field, judging having been completed earlier. The card that can be seen covering the entry number on the front of the engine being the prize that had been awarded.

Photo: Ian Bishop

Fowler 'Supremacy' (Works No.15375 - Reg. UUP 526 - New 1919) Originally hauled two big timber carriages in Gloucester but later converted for showman's use by Charles Openshaw of Reading and sold to Codonas, the Scottish showmen and travelled the Glasgow fairs. Seen here towing the Carnival Queen's float in 1960, after being purchased and restored by the Bishop Bros. of Burley, Craven Arms in the winter of 1959/60 from the well known engine owner Parky Bates.

Photo: Mr & Mrs Crowther

Tasker Traction Engine 'Lily of the Valley' (Works No.1718 - Reg. PU 5236 - New 1916) being a 5nhp single cylinder Class C type engine makes it a very fine little threshing engine, not too big but powerful for its size. The present day owner is Norman Wheeler, as he was back in 1960 when this photo was taken. He worked for Dick Woolley and is a fountain of knowledge and has helped with many a question.

Photo: Bill Ashley

Ruston, Proctor & Co. Single (Works No.52266 - Reg. CJ 4178 - New 1918) Owned by Dennis Smiths and outside the Greengrocers shop that he also owned in Sandford Avenue. There appears to be no sign of the driver though - was he attending to the fire or had he gone to his shop?

Photo: Bill Ashley

Garrett Tractor 'Rob Roy' (Works No.32981 - Reg. BJ 3282 - New 1917) seen here on Sandford Avenue, Church Stretton in 1961. Sold by E. Tanner of Caersws to G. Bowkley from Tenbury Wells in 1952 for a very brief spell in the timber trade. Then purchased in 1954 by F.R. Millward, Halesowen and later converted to the showman's type.

Photo: Heather Smith

Ruston & Hornsby Tractor (Works No.52766 - Reg. AW 4996 - New 1919) purchased by the then owner W. Griffiths of Much Wenlock who had done much work on it before 1960, seen here in the carnival procession of that year.

Photo: Mr & Mrs Crowther

Fowler Showman's Road Locomotive 'Supremacy' (Works No.15375 - Reg. UUP 526 - New 1919) owned by the Bishop Bros. of Burley, near Craven Arms. Since being in the ownership of the Bishop Bros. it had been repainted and lined to the high standard seen in this photo from 1961, our first rally.

Photo: Harry Turner

Fowler Showman's Road Loco 'Queen Mary' (Works No.15319 - Reg. FX 7850 - New 1918) Built to the order of the War Department but then sold as new in 1921 with the famous sister 'Kitchener' (alias 'The Iron Maiden'), without having worked on war service, to F.J. Barnes, a quarry owner from Portland. Both engines were sold in 1931 and 'Nellie', as it was then known, was converted locally to a showman's by R. Townsend of Weymouth for whom it worked for a further 10 years under its present name and was later purchased by W. Michael Salmon in 1951 and is seen here during the preparation of the 1961 rally.

Photo: Harry Turner

Clayton & Shuttleworth Tractor (Works No.49008 - Reg. VJ 5861 - New 1926) Not an uncommon make but this is believed to be the only surviving example, which was not actually sold until 1932 and may well be the last steam tractor supplied as new by any maker. After working for L. Evans of Treago, Hereford it was used for threshing by James Davies of Gladestry and then laid aside for many years before being purchased for restoration by W. Michael Salmon. Stood by the front wheel in this picture from 1961 are Dick Woolley (grey hair) and Charlie Spencer (black hair), both being steam engine contractors from South Shropshire.

Photo: Harry Turner

Garrett Tractor 'Countess' (Works No.32969 - Reg. BJ 3280 - New 1917) George Davies & Sons of Ludlow worked this tractor on stone haulage and threshing for 10 years before it passed to W.A. Bishop & Sons of Burley for threshing duties and was the special pride of Percy Bishop.

Photo: Harry Turner

Dennis Smith, and his son Richard, driving his Ruston, Proctor & Co. engine onto an almost empty rally field for the first ever County of Salop Steam Engine Society Rally to be held on Monday 7th August 1961. Dennis was Rally Organiser and Society Chairman and there were 18 engine entries. This fantastic colour picture is one of a set of 40 colour slides from 1961 donated to our Society Archivist, Mike Llewellyn, by Mr Harry Turner from Newtown.

Photo: Harry Turner

Ruston & Hornsby Tractor (Works No.52766 - Reg. AW 4996 - New 1919) New to C.I. Coxon of Bridgnorth, who used it for threshing and hauling of two trailers. It was also used for direct ploughing, an operation which figured more in makers catalogues than in the fields, at least as far as this country was concerned. But in 1959, after 10 years of idleness, it was purchased by the then owner, W. Griffiths of Much Wenlock.

Photo: Harry Turner

Ruston, Proctor & Co. Traction Engine (Works No.52266 - Reg. CJ 4178 - New 1918) This grand little engine was one of many built for hay-baling during the First World War and threshed for many seasons for Mr Charles James of Pen-y-Parc, near Clifford, Hereford, who looked after it so well that it still ran well when acquired by Dennis Smith, although much work was needed on the boiler.

Photo: Barry J. Finch

Marshall Roller (Works No. 65650 - Reg. BE 2227 - New 1914) Supplied new to the contractor Thomas H. Savage of Aberystwyth, as a tractor and converted to a roller in 1922. Purchased by Tom Davies of New Cross, Aberystwyth c1925 and then onto John Peter Jones of Abermule c1939 who owned the Buttington Road Rolling Company, where it finished its working life. Sold for £45 in 1958 for preservation to Jonathan Garman, Leintwardine, who was aged 19 at the time.

Photo: Harry Turner

Ransomes, Sims & Jefferies Traction Engine (Works No.15609 - Reg. CJ 4220 - New 1904) Originally used for threshing and later as a crane, with a temporary jib fitted to the rear coupling, before being found in a quarry at Oreton some years later by its then owner, Geoffrey Lee of Shrewsbury in 1956. It was in a bad state and was re-tubed before being steamed home. But after a spell in the well-known engine hospital at Burley, where it received replacement rear wheels, it has been able to steam many miles and has even been featured in a national newspaper.

Photo: Barry J. Finch

Ransomes, Sims & Jefferies Traction Engine (Works No.27524 - Reg. E 5123 - New 1918) This is a typical example of the large 7nhp threshing engines built by the Ipswich firm and widely used for heavy threshing and baling in all parts of the country. It was acquired by Vin Nash of Plealey from another Mr Nash (no connection) of Wednesfield. Considerable restoration work was done with further work continuing after this photo was taken in 1961.

Photo: Harry Turner

Aveling & Porter (8 tons) Road Roller (Works No.9264 - Reg. EJ 966 - New 1920) This engine is actually a convertible and could be made into a tractor by exchanging the rollers for wheels. It was new to Aberystwyth Rural District Council and worked for its successors, Cardiganshire County Council until 1957. Owned in 1961 by Vin Nash of Plealey.

Photo: Harry Turner

Sentinel DG tractor 'Queen Mary' (Works No.9236 - Reg. AAM 483) Built as a timber tractor and worked for Mickleover Transport Ltd and later became the Sentinel Works tractor with the timber winch removed. Pictured here at the 1961 rally, when it was owned by Cliff James of Kingswinford, but with the registration plate from another DG timber tractor (Works No.9097), which he also owned, and apparently was not an unusual occurrence for Cliff James!

Photo: Harry Turner

A rare colour photo of Dick Woolley's Sentinel S4 (Works No.9346 - Reg. CXB 783) taken at our Church Stretton Rally in 1961. Note that the tar tank and spray bar have been removed when compared to the earlier carnival picture. The waggon was rallied just once like this before being sold with a spare boiler and engine in 1962 to the Philadelphia Naval Yard in the USA. It re-emerged in 1990 at the National Transport Museum in St Louis, Missouri, where it still resides.

Photo: Harry Turner

Super Sentinel Tractor (Works No.6695 - Reg. EX 1638 - New 1926) New to a brewery in Great Yarmouth as a Waggon, but then acquired by The Messrs. Billington & Sons of Liverpool, who traded as Criddle & Co, about 1930 and converted to a tractor. It worked for them on Liverpool docks hauling grain until 1959. Seen here at the 1961 rally, owned by A. Williamson from Endon, Stoke-on-Trent but unfortunately it's not been out for a number of years now.

Photo: Barry J. Finch

Fowler D5 Road Locomotive 'Cynorthwywr', (Welsh for 'Helper') (Works No.15787 - Reg. EP 2398 - New 1924) Originally intended as a road engine when new to Ellis Jones of Newtown, Mid-Wales, but went threshing in later years when in the ownership of The Messrs. Tanner of Caersws and was well up to the "double work" i.e. driving a threshing drum and a baler. The front wheels are from a Sentinel Super Tractor and were put on when the spokes in the original wheels became loose.

Photo: Barry J. Finch

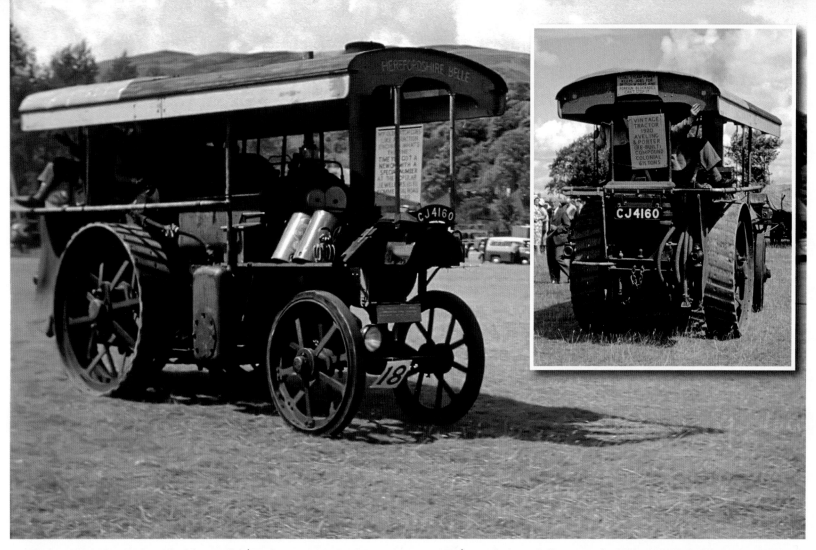

Aveling & Porter Tractor 'Herefordshire Belle' (Works No.9225 - Reg. CJ 4160 - New 1920) Supplied originally to Hereford CC, then worked for C & J Smith of Bromyard. Later purchased by C.F. Smith, a clock maker from Hereford. Worried about safety, he had a rail put around it and a piece of wood behind the flywheel just in case it should burst! Like many others of that time, he was worried about the threat of the atom bomb so went to live in the remotest part of the Brecon Mountains.

Photo: Harry Turner

Sentinel Super Tractor (Works No.6695 - Reg. EX 1638) converted from a waggon. Here we see Alan Williamson en route to the Church Stretton Rally in 1962, coming past the railway station when the A49 ran directly through the centre of Shrewsbury. Also seen on the left of the photo opposite.

Photo: Harry Turner

Three Sentinels from the 1962 engine line up that are not seen much these days. *Entry 14* - Standard Sentinel Steam Waggon 'Shrewsbury Belle' (Works No.2307 - Reg. AW 4693 - New 1919) Owned by S.L., D.L. and P.H. Wedgwood, Kidsgrove. *Entry 15* - Super Sentinel Tractor (Works No.7527 - Reg. MP 5939 - New 1928) Owned by W.G. Powell, Mold. *Entry 16* - Super Sentinel Tractor (Works No.6695 - Reg. EX 1638 - New 1926) Owned by A. Williamson, Endon.

Photo: Harry Turner

Burrell (6nhp) Agricultural Engine (Works No.2003 - Reg. YA 509 - New 1897) Pictured outside the entrance to the railway goods yard prior to the 1962 Church Stretton Rally. The engine was new to a farm in Dorset and later sold into Somerset, before ending its working days in a Bristol scrap yard and rescued in the late 1950's by Richard Wilcox of Stonehouse, Gloucestershire. Here named 'Firefly', but previously named 'Diamond Queen' which has been reinstated in recent years.

Photo: Barry J. Finch

Roller Corner at the 1962 rally. *Entry 31* - Fowler Compound (Works No.19047 - Reg. UX 8669 - New 1931) owned by W.A. Bishop & Sons, Burley. *Entry 32* - Clayton & Shuttleworth (Works No.46688 - Reg. EP 3137 - New 1914) owned by G. Minshall, Bridgnorth. *Entry 35* - Fowler D2 Compound (Works No.13453 - Reg. EP 3138 - New 1912) convertible roller, owned by Buttington Road Rolling Co. Ltd, Welshpool. *Entry 36* - Marshall Single (Works No.82389 - Reg. UO 2835 - New 1927) owned by R.M. Woolley, Bucknell. Note the consecutive registrations of entries 32 and 35, being first registered together in 1920 when in the ownership of J. Peter Jones of Newtown, Mid-Wales. The Marshall and both Fowlers were still working machines at this time.

Photo: Harry Turner

This fine picture of the Bishop brothers with 'Supremacy' at the 1962 rally clearly shows what a fantastic restoration they had done. From the left is Leslie, holding the Best Engine at Rally Cup, Cyril and Percy, with the Best Tractor Cup for his Garrett 'Countess'. Percy was sadly killed a week later while welding an underground water tank which had contained petrol some 20 years previous. The heat of the weld had driven petrol vapour out of the seams and rust, resulting in the tank exploding.

Photo: Mr & Mrs Crowther

Foster Compound Traction Engine 'Winnie' (Works No.12539 - Reg. MA 5730 - New 1910) at the 1963 rally. New to The Messrs. Bonell of Audlem, then William Barlow of High Legh and worked until 1950 before being restored to its original condition. Later owned by Jim Dakin of Goostrey, Cheshire, and with the addition of rubber tyres, is possibly the most travelled traction engine in preservation, with threshing box and living van in tow.

Photo: Mr & Mrs Crowther

A selection of engines parked up in the railway station yard prior to the 1964 rally. Ted Jones' Marshall portable (Works No.79936) in the foreground and then left to right in the background is Norman Wheeler's Tasker 'Lily of the Valley' (Works No.1718 - Reg. PU 5236), Les Lambe's Foster (Works No.14514 - Reg. CA 8534), Alan Williamson's Super Sentinel Tractor (Works No.6695 - Reg. EX 1638), Tom Henderson's Ransomes Sims & Jefferies portable (Works No.20539) and his Fowler Traction Engine 'Dreadnought', later named 'Pride of the Wye' (Works No.9225 - Reg. CF 3795) and Painter's Garrett engine (Works No.29764 - Reg. AC 9326).

Photo: Barry J. Finch

Ransomes, Sims & Jefferies Traction Engine (Works No.15609 - CJ 4220) Geoff Lee looking as black as ever after the 1961 rally turning off the A49 by the Dorrington sand and gravel pit, heading for Vin Nash's at Plealey. When looking at this picture, Mike Llewellyn, our Society Archivist was surprised to identify the two boys on bikes are in actual fact his brother, on the right, and himself on the left.

Photo: Heather Smith

Clayton & Shuttleworth Roller (Works No.46688 - Reg. EP 3137) pictured here at the 1965 Church Stretton Rally. New in 1914 to John Peter Jones of Newtown, Powys, and eventually passing to the Buttington Road Rolling Company of Welshpool and then finally purchased by S. & G. Minshall from Bridgnorth, who still own it. Unfortunately it's not been seen in public for some 20 years.

Photo: Norman Owen

A very nice colour photo at an unknown location of Geoff Lee, nearest the camera, on 'Salopian' his Ransomes Sims & Jefferies engine. He always said that this was the original colour scheme of the engine.

Photo: Mr & Mrs Crowther

Wallis & Steevens Tractor (Works No.2811) New in 1905 to S. Smith, a Coal Merchant from Newport, Shropshire. After several owners, including commandeering in the 1914 war, it came to Ivor Dobbs of Longhope, Gloucestershire and was registered AD 7460. Purchased in 1961 by Derek Hackett of Bridstow, Ross-on-Wye. Seen here at our 1964 rally, restoration had been done on behalf of the owner by Bishop Bros. of Burley, Craven Arms. The driver was Iwan Jones of Cardiff.

Photo: David Bradbury

Burrell Road Loco (Works No.2646 - Reg. AD 8923) New to Hawkes Bros of Gloucester in 1904 for road haulage and in later years was the largest engine to go threshing in Radnorshire, with the Price family at Llowes, near Hay-on-Wye. The inset photo shows it at Llowes in 1959 before it was restored. Pictured here at the 1965 rally, when it was owned by Mr G.M. Webster of West Kirby, with Reg Wheeler on the footplate and John Fisher on the far side.

Photo: David Bradbury   Inset Photo: Barry J. Finch

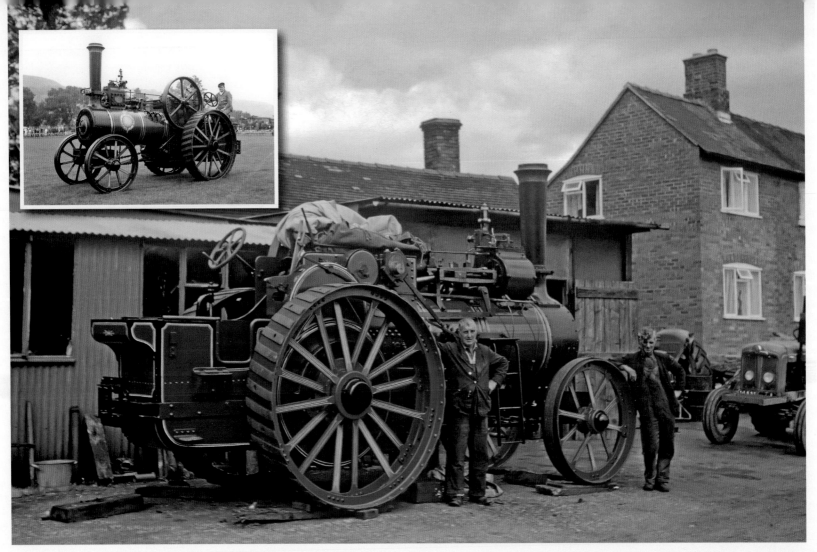

Ransomes Sims & Jefferies (7nhp) Traction Engine (Works No.26952 - Reg. AY 9704) New in 1916 and worked in Leicestershire, where its ability to cope with "double work", threshing and baling, would be utilised to the full. Later purchased by Eric Lawrence of Mathon, Malvern and used to sterilise soil for a nursery near Malvern. Pictured at Bishop's yard, Burley in 1966 with Cyril (left) and Les who had completely renovated the engine for Eric. Inset shows the engine at the 1966 rally.

Photo: Mr & Mrs Crowther · Inset Photo: Barry J. Finch

Standard Sentinel Steam Waggon (Works No.3899 - Reg. ET 1969 - New 1921) Photographed in commercial condition in 1966; note the angle of the front wheels. Owned at the time by L. Mellor of Chapel-en-le-Frith. This Waggon was used until 1966 for internal transport by Brown-Bayley Steels Ltd of Sheffield. They survived on this work for many years after disappearing from the roads, due to their ability to enter hot parts of the steel works and carry hot metal without risk of fire. Seen here turning into Beaumont Road, Church Stretton, heading towards the rally field.

Photo: Barry J. Finch

Burrell Showman's Tractor 'Peter Pan' (Works No.3433 - Reg. AH 0108) New at the 1912 Smithfield Show to The Messrs. Kemp of Aldershot for timber haulage, and despite being so small, was later converted to Showman's for Mrs J. Cole and carried three of the lighter loads of a Scenic Railway. Arrived in Shropshire by rail in 1965 and the last engine to be loaded at Lavenham, Suffolk before the station closed. Owned by W.M. Salmon of Llandrindod Wells at the time and believed to be the only engine unloaded at Church Stretton Station. Seen here at the 1966 Church Stretton rally.

Photo: Mr & Mrs Crowther

Burrell Scenic Road Loco 'Winston Churchill' (Works No.3909 - Reg. NR 965) Originally owned by A. Holland of Swadlincote and called 'Pride of the Road'. Acquired by Mr Middleton and renamed 'Winston Churchill'. Seen here at the last Church Stretton Rally in 1968 when owned by F.P. Middleton of Hartlebury, being helped by Iwan Jones and his Ransomes, Sims & Jefferies Traction Engine (Works No.31136 - Reg. DM 3048 - New 1920).

Photo: Harry Turner

Entry No 26 - S-type Sentinel Waggon (Works No.9192 - Reg. CML 781 - New 1935) Hauled coal for Tottenham & District Gas Co. and kept on the road until after WW2. At the time, they were far ahead of other vehicles of similar capacity with a top speed in excess of 40mph. This Waggon was known as 'The Bomb', as the throttle had a tendency to get stuck, so the owner had a piece of string tied to the pedal to pull it shut. Then owned by G.B. King of Highbridge, Somerset.

Entry No 27 - S-type Sentinel Waggon (Works No.8884 - Reg. TJ 3319 - New 1933) New to Rainford Potteries and later passed to George Davies of Liverpool, for whom it worked until 1958. Rated to carry a legal load of 8tons with another 5tons on a trailer, they often took a good deal more. Entered in the 2011 Historic Commercial Vehicle Run to Brighton and covered the 430 miles on 18cwts of coal. At the time good coal was less than a quarter of its present price, these were very economical Waggons in their day. Owned by A. Williamson of Endon, Stoke-on-Trent.

Photo: Harry Turner

Sentinel S-type Waggon (Works No.9075 - Reg. BEV 467 - New 1934) First owned by Brown Bros of Chelmsford then the Castle Firebrick Co., Buckley, Flintshire, where it was later partly dismantled for spares for their other two Waggons. All three survive in preservation and for a time were owned by Dick Woolley of Bucknell. Purchased in an incomplete state in 1965 and rebuilt by The Messrs. Brook, Hirst & Marsden of Huddersfield, the owners at the time. Also seen on the left of the photo on the opposite page prior to being sign written.

Photo: Harry Turner

BISHOPS CASTLE
RALLY, 1970

2/-

BISHOP'S CASTLE

After last minute problems with a new venue ended in the 1969 rally having to be cancelled, a new home was found at Bishop's Castle for the 1970 rally and with the new venue came the decision to also make it a two day rally.

The early 70's saw the original showman's engines of the Church Stretton days slowly fading away. Mike Salmon, who had been the Steam Engine Section Secretary up until 1971/72, had not been very well and had sold two of his four engines, 'Queen Mary' and the 5 ton Foden wagon. Luckily Frank Lythgoe's fine collection of showman's engines had begun to grow and they became the main stay of the Grand Parade. However nothing will ever replace the memory of 'Supremacy' and 'Queen Mary' as

immortalised in David Bradbury's poem, which has itself become very much a part of the Grand Parade.

The evening time in Bishop's Castle saw the showman's engines come to life, with each pub in the town having an engine and fairground organ parked outside. This made a fantastic spectacle with a fine party atmosphere.

During the years at Bishop's Castle came the 21st Anniversary, which was celebrated with a road run from the former venue in Church Stretton back to Bishop's Castle, and the 25th Anniversary, which was also celebrated with a road run but this time from the old Sentinel Works in Shrewsbury.

The 1970 Grand Parade - a true tradition of the County of Salop Steam Engine Society. For the ninth and, sadly, last time the parade is lead by Fowlers 'Supremacy' and 'Queen Mary'. Followed by 'Enterprise', Mike Salmons Burrell Tractor 'Peter Pan' and his Clayton & Shuttleworth Tractor 'Apollo'.

Photo: Harry Turner

Fowler Showman's Road Loco 'Enterprise' (Works No.14588 - Reg. DO 1932 - New 1916) Was a preservation conversion to showman's having had a working life on haulage. Payloads of 40 tons were quite common for this type of engine, and often over difficult roads. The owner, F. Hackney, Sandbach is stood at the back of the engine in this photo from 1970 and attended four rallies up to 1973 but unfortunately it has not been seen out for many years.

Photo: Harry Turner

Clayton & Shuttleworth Tractor 'Apollo' (Works No.49008 - Reg. VJ 5861 - New 1926) This was the last Clayton tractor to be built in Lincoln and mostly used for threshing and timber haulage by J. Davies of Gladestry and very quiet when on the road. Repainted Green since its last rally in 1968 when owned by W. Michael Salmon, Craven Arms and assisted by Charlie Spencer.

Photo: Harry Turner   Inset Photo: Barry J. Finch

Foden 5-ton Wagon and Trailer 'Pride of Burley' (Works No.5078 - Reg. M 7124 - New 1914) Originally used by the Royal Naval Air Service at Devonport for the transport of aircraft but later passed to Bristow Bros. of Hereford. It was recovered by Mike Salmon from a sand pit in Herefordshire in 1962, having been set in concrete to belt drive machinery. Seen here in 1970, the Foden trailer is contemporary, the wagon being intended to work with such a trailer to carry 8-10 tons. The inset shows Mike Salmon working on the wagon at Burley c1964.

Photo: Harry Turner

Fowler Traction Engine (Works No.9225 - Reg. CF 3795 - New 1901) First owned by the Jockey Club, Newmarket and then William Tilbrook of Thurlow, Suffolk who used it for contract threshing and later by his son until 1947. Purchased by Tom Henderson of Whitney-on-Wye and first rallied at Church Stretton in 1964, with much heavy restoration work being undertaken. Seen here in 1970 when the engine was not lined out and carrying its former name of 'Dreadnought'.

Photo: Harry Turner

Sentinel DG Tractor (Works No.9236 - Reg. AAM 483 - New 1936) seen here with no winch, and Sentinel DG Tractor (Works No.9097 - Reg. ARE 195 - New 1934). Pictured in 1970 when both tractors were owned by Cliff James from Newport, Shropshire. No.9097 having recently been extensively restored by Ted Proctor.

Photo: Harry Turner

Clayton & Shuttleworth Roller (Works No.48944 - Reg. EP 2574 - New 1924) New to Corfields of Abermule and worked mainly in Montgomeryshire, until it was purchased for preservation in 1968 by its then lady owner Mrs Elizabeth Mason of Newport, Shropshire; famous for her flower covered overalls. Seen here in 1970.

Photo: Mr & Mrs Crowther

Aveling & Porter Tractor (Works No.9225 - Reg. CJ 4160 - New 1920) Remember the strange looking Aveling with the crash bars earlier in the book? Well this is the same little engine pictured in 1970. This KND Colonial tractor was new to Herefordshire County Council for hauling road stone and passed to C. & J. Smith of Pencombe for threshing in 1937. Acquired in semi-derelict condition in 1967 and restored by the new owner D.C. Hackett of Ross-on-Wye.

Photo: Harry Turner

Burrell Traction Engine 'Earl Haig' (Works No.3812 - Reg. AW 9198 - New 1919) New to Major Benson of Much Wenlock, this engine passed to The Messrs. Jones Bros. of Westbury, Shropshire and worked until 1947 threshing and baling. It then lay derelict for many years at Castle Caereinion Station until purchased in 1964 by George Bowkley of Tenbury Wells. Pictured here in 1971, but now carries its original name 'Haig'.

Photo: Harry Turner

Foden 5 ton Wagon 'Pride of Edwin' or 'Foden's Foden' as it was always called (Works No.6368 - Reg. M 8118 - New 1916) Delivered new to Portsea Island Gas Light Co. as a three-way tipper and had a long working life, before being purchased by Fodens and appearing in the Foden Centenary Parade in 1956. It was subsequently brought up to exhibition standard and shown at rallies throughout the country, as seen here in 1971.

Photo: Tom Henderson

Burrell Traction Engine 'General C.R. DeWet' (Works No.2512 - Reg. TB 2846 - New 1902) Worked every season threshing for The Messrs. Isaac Ball & Sons Contractors of Wharles, Lancashire until 1948. Unused for several years, then purchased for restoration in 1964 by David Goddard, seen here in 1971 and is still in the same family today.

Photo: Tom Henderson

Ransomes, Sims & Jefferies Traction Engine (Works No.31136 - Reg. DM 3048 - New 1920) Bought off the makers stand at the 1920 Royal Show at Doncaster by Rt. Hon. Lord Mostyn to drive the sawmill at Mostyn Hall, Flintshire for the next 43 years. The road gearing was still like new when purchased in 1965 by Iwan Jones of St Mellons, Cardiff. Seen here in 1972.

Photo: Tom Henderson

Super Sentinel Waggon (Works No.8393 - Reg. DX 9048) New in 1930 to William Brown & Co, a miller in Ipswich. It finished it working life with Wingham Engineering in Kent, before being taken over in 1970 by H.M.S. Sultan, the Royal Navy's School of Marine Engineering at Gosport. It is maintained by a small group of volunteers and was on a tour of Wales in 1972. It came again in 1986 and 87 and twice after that including the special Sentinel display of 2002 for our 40th rally.

Photo: Harry Turner

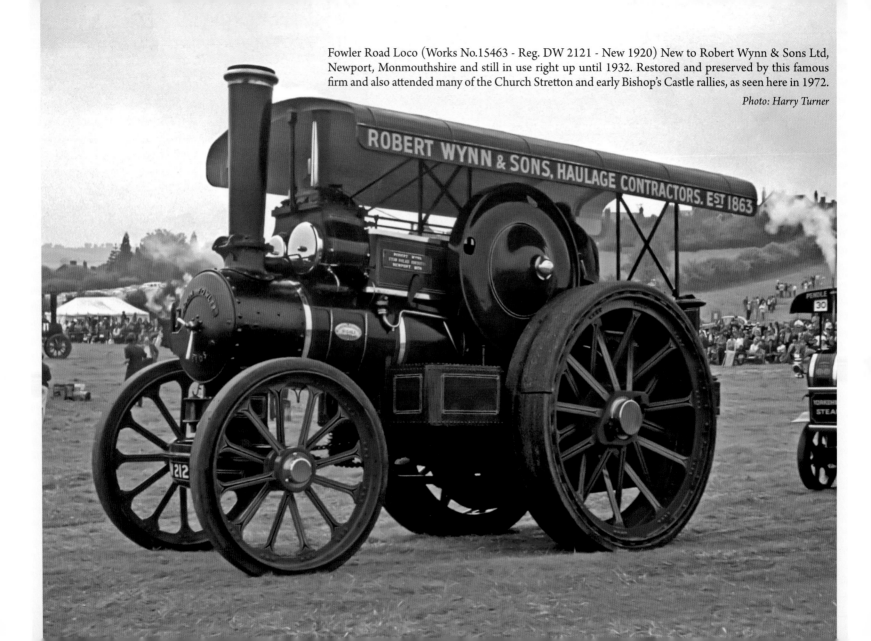

Fowler Road Loco (Works No.15463 - Reg. DW 2121 - New 1920) New to Robert Wynn & Sons Ltd, Newport, Monmouthshire and still in use right up until 1932. Restored and preserved by this famous firm and also attended many of the Church Stretton and early Bishop's Castle rallies, as seen here in 1972.

Photo: Harry Turner

Yorkshire Patent Steam Wagon Co, 3ton wagon 'Pendle Queen' (Works No.940 - Reg. U 4245) New to Clayton and Co. Engineers, Leeds in 1917 and later purchased by an adjacent company, Robinson & Birdsell Ltd and used for scrap metal haulage, but finally scrapped itself in 1936. Saved from a scrapyard on Hunslet Moor in 1969 by Mr Tom Varley, Gisburn, who also owned it at the time of this 1972 photo.

Photo: Harry Turner

Aveling & Porter Roller (Works No.3586 - Reg. MA 7890 - New 1895) Supplied new to Sefton District Highway Board, Lancashire and then later worked for the Lancashire Road Rolling Company of Altrincham, Cheshire. Passing to Cardiganshire County Council in 1927 where it worked until 1960. It was saved from scrap at the very last minute by Mike Salmon and transported to Ludlow on David Webster's low loader and pushed to Burley by Dennis Smith with his 7hp Burrell 2646. Owned in this 1972 photo by W.W. Foxall & G. Minshall, Bridgnorth who had restored it at Burley.

Photo: Tom Henderson

Burrell Showman's (8hp) Road Loco. 'Dreadnought' (Works No.3093 - Reg. AY 9682) New in April 1909 to Holland's Amusement Caterers of Mile End, London. Lay derelict in Oxfordshire in the 1950's and later bought from W.H. Dorman of Nottingham by Frank Lythgoe of Lymm, Cheshire in February 1973 and is pictured here in 1974 prior to extensive restoration work being done. This was the beginning of a new era for the Grand Parades at our rallies, as 'Supremacy' and 'Queen Mary' never attended again.

Photo: Harry Turner

Foden D Type Tractor (Works No.13784 - Reg. UX 9728) New in 1932 to Ashworths of Newport, Shropshire who eventually traded it in for a new Foden diesel. Fodens sold it to Birmingham showman, Randall Monte who very soon sold it to Henry Holland of Market Drayton, Shropshire. Purchased in 1945 by W.A. Bishop & Sons of Burley and preserved in 1960. By 1974, and in this picture, the tractor was with Jack Crabtree of Sutton Coldfield, but in the care of Bob Bailey, who now owns it.

Photo: Harry Turner

Yorkshire Patent Steam Wagon Co. 2ton Wagon 'Pendle Maid' (Works No.117 - Reg. CA 170) New to Hon. J.C. Best of Vivod Hall, Llangollen in 1905. The chassis was found on a farm by Mike Jones of Llanbedr in 1970. He informed Tom Varley and it was subsequently purchased and rebuilt. Owned at the time of this 1975 photo by Tom Varley, Gisburn. The gents on the engine are Harry Turner and Charlie Bowen, both crew members of Don Pritchards Fowler roller.

Photo: Alan Johnson

Sentinel S4 (Works No.8942 - Reg. ATN 320) New to McEwan's Breweries in Newcastle-upon-Tyne, eventually finishing its working life as a tar tanker for Robert Bridson & Sons of Neston, Cheshire. Purchased by David Webster and restored by the 1970 rally. On the left is a rare colour image of David Webster's Sentinel S6 (seen opposite) still painted green as it was when first purchased in 1973 from R. Parkinson of Exeter. Seen here in the famous Bishop Bros. yard at Burley in 1973.

Photo: Alan Johnson

Sentinel S6 3-way Tipper Waggon (Works No.8821 - Reg. BRF 200) Seen here in 1975, 2 years after the photo opposite, the prototype 'S' Type six-wheeler, and only the 6th shaft drive built, was new to Tarmac of Wolverhampton in 1933 for road stone haulage. Then to Cambridge Gas Works for bulk coke transport, followed by A.R.C. of Nottingham and finally purchased by R. Parkinson of Exeter for preservation and rebuilding. Later purchased by David Webster in 1973.

Photo: Michael Llewellyn

Marshall (4hp) Portable Engine (Works No.79936) New to Mr T. Jones of Llanfair Caereinion in 1925 and purchased in 1963 by the present owner for preservation after it being left neglected for many years. We believe that this photo, at our 1975 rally, was possibly the first time a portable engine had been seen being pulled by horses at a rally. Owner: Mr G.E. Jones (Ted), Shrewsbury.

Photo: David Bradbury

Burrell Showman's (7hp) Road Locomotive 'Princess Marina' (Works No.3847 - Reg. CL 4483 - New 1912) Originally built under a different number and was a high working pressure test engine until 1920 when it was rebuilt, re-numbered and sold to showman Hannah Parkin of Norwich. It worked for John Barker during the war pulling a 30ton roller used in airfield construction, later sold for threshing. Bought in 1960 and restored by the owners in this 1975 photo, J. & D. Walker of Minsterley.

Photo: Harry Turner

Marshall Traction Engine (Works No.69326 - Reg. BD 5525 - New 1915) This big 8nhp traction engine was owned by The Messrs. Kimbell of Boughton, Northamptonshire who had an extensive threshing business. Driven by Mr E.E. Kimble at some of this countries earliest rallies ever held, back in the 1950's. Seen in this photo, from the mid 1970's, owned by W. Sambrook of Newport, Shropshire.

Photo: Michael Llewellyn

Burrell Showman (8hp) Engine 'His Lordship' (Works No.3444 - Reg. CK 4303 - New 1913) Originally built for Greens of Glasgow and went on to work for Green's of Preston. It changed hands again in about 1936, going to Silcocks of Warrington but was purchased for preservation in 1949 by Tom Albert and then by Tom Varley in 1975 and completely rebuilt, the result of which can be seen in this 1976 photo.

Photo: David Bradbury

Dick Woolley was still dredging ponds and lakes up until 1976 with his pair of BB1 Ploughing Engines. The left photo shows Dick on engine No. 15194 (Reg. FX 6820) being assisted by one of our former Vice Chairmen, Andrew Semple (in the hat). This job, on a farm at Montford Bridge, was unfortunately to be Dick's last due to poor health.

Photo: Colin Matthews

This lower photo shows the second engine, the 'pull back' engine (Works No.15195 - Reg. FX 6821) The boy on the engine is Dick Woolley's son.

Photo: Colin Matthews

(*Left*) Robey Express Tractor (Works No.43388 - Reg. VL 983) New in 1929 to Clarks of Erith, Kent as a high speed tractor for stone haulage. Purchased by Thomas Davies of Craven Arms and passed to Richard (Dick) Woolley of Bucknell in 1938 and used throughout the war for threshing around South Shropshire. This was Dick Woolley's first engine and he went on to own over 70 engines at various times. Seen here in 1976 when owned by Tom Varley of Gisburn, Yorkshire.

(*Right*) Yorkshire Wagon WG Model (Works No.2004 - Reg. UA 1163) New to Leeds Electric Depot in 1927 as an articulated vehicle, for hauling electricity cables.

Photo: Alan Johnson

Burrell Showman's (8hp) Road Loco 'Dolphin' (Works No.4030 - Reg. FA 2316 - New 1925) New to William Davies of Stoke-on-Trent and the last to be built by Burrells for showmen. Purchased by John Shaw of Sheffield in 1927 and later sold to Mr. H.J. Wallis of Seaforth, Liverpool, finally acquired for preservation in 1959. Pictured here, in 1977 on its first visit to one of our rallies, owned by Frank Lythgoe.

Photo: Trevor Smallbone

Foden 'D' Type Tractor (Works No.13762 - Reg. VN 2911 - New 1931) Supplied new to the North Riding County Council and used with two Foden trailers for hauling road stone until 1934. It was kept for standby duties until 1958, when it was sold for preservation to Mr D. Thackeray of Malton and acquired by the present owner, Mr I. Jones of Cardiff, in January 1972. Seen here in 1978.

Photo: Trevor Smallbone

Fowler (7hp) Road Loco (Works No.15376 - Reg. MA 5656) Bought new in 1919 by Robert Bridson & Sons of Neston, Cheshire for general haulage during the last war, the engine was used to haul Sherman tanks from Liverpool Docks to Donnington, ships propellers around Merseyside and many heavy wartime loads, as well as stone and tar-spraying duties in North and Mid Wales. Seen here in 1978, when owned by George Bridson.

Photo: Trevor Smallbone

Garrett Showman's Type Tractor 'Rob Roy' (Works No.32981 - Reg. BJ 3282 - New 1917) Seen earlier in the book, it went to our first rally in 1961. It was converted to showman's spec by the Millward Brothers in the early 1960's. Purchased in 1973 by Mr Les Bishop of Burley, Craven Arms and is seen here at our 1978 rally.

Photo: Bryan Roberts

McLaren Showman's (10hp) Road Locomotive 'Goliath' (Works No.1623 - Reg. DH 2482) New to the War Department in 1917 and saw active service hauling heavy guns in France during the 1914-18 war. Converted to showman's specification after the war and used for the rest of its working life by Pat Collins of Bloxwich and came to Shrewsbury Fairs up until 1956. This picture shows it in 1979 during its first appearance at our rallies, when owned by Frank Lythgoe, Lymm.

Photo: Mr & Mrs Crowther

Sentinel S8 Steam Waggon (Works No.9105 - Reg.UJ 3652 - New 1934) Originally a Sentinel demonstration wagon, it was rebuilt from a pile of scrap in 1970/71 and has been rallied extensively since. It's the only surviving shaft drive 8 wheeler known to exist from a total of 9 built. Owned by the famous Sentinel owner, Mr E.N. Shone from London, at the time of this photo in 1979.

Photo: David Bradbury

Burrell Showman's (6hp) Engine 'Fermoy' (Works No.3090 - Reg. OH 5022) New to Pool & Bosco Showmen of Birmingham in 1909. Sold to Mrs Shepherd of Birmingham in 1921, then W.A. Bishop & Sons of Burley in 1927 who used it for threshing until selling it to R.M. Woolley of Bucknell for threshing. After two more owners it was bought once again by Mr Woolley for preservation and sold to Mr J. Miles in 1969, seen here in 1979 with its former owner and driver, Les Bishop.

Photo: Alan Johnson

Garrett (4hp) Showman's type conversion 'Lady Sarah' (Works No.33074 - Reg. BJ 3451) Converted from a tractor by Les Lambe of Bromsgrove and owned by Peter Timmis of Shrewsbury, at the time of this photo in 1979 during its first year out.

Photo: Mr & Mrs Crowther

Ransomes, Sims & Jefferies Portable Engine (Works No.20539) New to Lord Hereford's Estate in 1908 and used until 1940. After which it was sold to Mr Brewer of Hereford who used it for steaming pig swill until 1962, when it was purchased by the current owner, Mr T. Henderson of Whitney-on-Wye, and is seen here at one of many visits to our rallies during the 1970's.

Photo: Harry Turner

1982 was our 21ˢᵗ Anniversary and to celebrate we held a road run from Church Stretton to Bishop's Castle. In this picture we see David Parry (left) and Norman Owen, our Chairman at the time, holding the starting bell used to send the engines off at 2 minute intervals. On the right, in the overalls, is Ewan Lloyd-Jones with the Sentinel DG4 Waggon (Works No.8122 - Reg. OF 5783) owned in 1982 and still in commercial use by Lloyd-Jones Bros., Ruthin.

Photo: David Bradbury

Ruston, Proctor & Co. (5hp) Traction Engine 'Corn Maiden' (Works No.52266 - Reg. CJ 4178) Dennis Smith sold the engine in 1971 and then it was re-sold to B. Wilkins of Langport, Somerset in 1972 who fitted a new firebox in 1976. It was very nice indeed to see the engine once owned by our founder, Dennis Smith, back in Church Stretton for the 21st Anniversary in 1982.

Photo: David Bradbury

Fowler Traction Engine 'Pride of the Wye' (Works No.9225 - Reg. CF 3795) owned by Tom Henderson. Tom Tong is driving and Tom Henderson's son, David, is steering. Seen here just south of Church Stretton, making their way to Bishop's Castle on the road run held in 1982 to mark our 21st Anniversary. The trailer, also owned by Tom Henderson, is a Laker made near London.

Photo: Tom Henderson

Burrell Showman's Road Locomotive 'Perseverance The Second' (Works No.3483 - Reg. WR 9110) Supplied new in 1913 to Harniess Bros. of Swinton, near Doncaster staying in their ownership until 1944 when it was sold to Mrs J. Cole of Chichester, Sussex and used until 1947. Finally sold for preservation in 1953 to J.N. Gilbey of Yeovil, Somerset. Pictured opposite the Powis Arms, Lydbury North during the Anniversary Road Run in 1982.

Photo: Harry Turner

Aveling & Porter (4hp) Convertible Tractor 'Molly Pugh' (Works No.9181 - Reg. EP 1649) New to Montgomeryshire C.C. in 1920. Used as a roller for many years before laying for many years inside the Cambrian Foundry and then in the council yard in Newtown, Powys. Purchased by Geoff Lee of Shrewsbury and restored to working order by Hughie Smith. Seen here in 1982 when owned by Mrs M. Smith of Wellington, Shropshire.

Photo: Tom Henderson

Fowler Showman's Road Locomotive 'Repulse' (Works No.15652 - Reg. CU 977 - New 1920) Another famous name in Showman's road locomotives, this engine was not rallied as much as its twin sister 'Renown'. Seen here in 1984 when owned by Mr P. Startup of Knutsford, Cheshire.

Photo: John Brooks

Foster (10hp) Showman's Scenic Road Locomotive 'The Leader' (Works No.14446 - Reg. DH 4593) Supplied second hand by Fosters in 1927 to Pat Collins and remained in continuous service until 1958. It was the last engine to appear at Nottingham Goose Fair in 1957 and the first to return in 1981, where it worked for three days driving a modern ride. Purchased by the present day owner, Mr W.T. Hunt of Oldbury, West Midlands in 1960 and seen here in 1983.

Photo: David Bradbury

1984 Grand Parade - the year of the miners strike. The only coal we could get was Daw Mill Steam Coal which was good but more than a bit smokey! In front of 'Goliath' (left) and 'Dolphin' (right) is, from the left, Frank Lythgoe, owner of the two engines, David Bradbury, our Commentator, and Norman Owen, our Chairman since 1961. Unfortunately this was to be Norman's last rally as he sadly passed away in February 1985.

Photo: Bob Carter

Aveling & Porter (10tons) Road Roller 'Rosetta' (Works No.9024 - Reg. NT 2019) New to Shropshire C.C. in 1919 and spent most of its working life in the Oakengates area and retired in 1956. Mrs Bates, a retired Headmistress, financed the early preservation of the engine at the Klondyke Mill, Derbyshire. An extensive renovation had been carried out by the time of this 1984 photo by her owners, Jim & Joan Cook, Lea Cross, Shrewsbury.

Photo: John Brooks

To celebrate the 25th Anniversary of our Society, and 25th Rally, we organised a Sentinel road run from the Sentinel Works in Shrewsbury back to the rally field at Bishop's Castle.

Top row: All the waggons lined up outside the works, we blocked the A49 trunk road for some time.

Photos: David Bradbury and Steve Meredith

Bottom row: Various waggons set off past the old tin sheet part of the works that is now demolished and replaced with a Morrisons supermarket, which does have a very nice plaque in the entrance to the store remembering the old Sentinel Waggon Works.

Photos: Harry Turner

Sentinel DG4 Timber Tractor 'Brutus' (Works No.8756 - Reg. VN 4294) New to an owner in Northallerton, Yorkshire then Dick Woolley of Bucknell by 1949, who used it for heating tar tanks and snow ploughing. Sold on to a timber company in Weston-super-Mare and then purchased for Robert Bloom, Bressingham, Diss, Norfolk as a wedding present from his Father and rebuilt by the Bressingham Steam Museum in 1980. Seen here in 1986 on its only visit to our rally.

Photo: David Bradbury

Sentinel DG Tractor (Works No.9097 - Reg. ARE 195) Remember the registration plate had been to the first rally but on 'Queen Mary', the red tractor! Cliff James purchased it in 1945 for timber work then it was restored in the 60's and first steamed in 1969. Seen here in 1986, and still under the same ownership, at the top of Asterley Bank, near Pontesbury on the main road to Bishop's Castle.

Photo: Michael Llewellyn

Fowler Roller (Works No.14333 - New 1914) Supplied to Tewkesbury Rural District Council then sold through various hands before being owned by Dick Woolley of Bucknell in 1951. Purchased in 1956 by Don Pritchard of Hendomen, Montgomery and used commercially up until 1970, and for preservation in later years as seen in this photo from 1989 when it had just been repainted and the canopy rebuilt to look as near to the original as possible.

Photo: David Bradbury

Sentinel Standard Waggon 'The Old Man' (Presented as Works No.1170 - Reg. V 513) An early model supplied to C.H. Butt of Weston-super-Mare to deliver quarry products, up until 1927 when it went into disuse. Purchased in 1967 by E. Shone of Cricklewood, London, but it was minus many parts including the engine and boiler. So it was rebuilt using parts from two others found in Scotland, and is seen here in 1989 on its first year out after the rebuild.

Photo: Mr & Mrs Crowther

Fowler BB1 Ploughing Engine (Works No.15333 - Reg. AL 9855 - New 1919) A special arena event at our Bishop's Castle rallies was the ploughing engine demonstration, seen here with Jonathan Garman's engine winching Tom Henderson's Fowler, 'Pride of the Wye', across the main arena in 1989. Jonathan has been a life long steam man, entering his Marshall roller in the 1961 rally aged only 19.

Photo: John Brooks

Garrett (4hp) Showman's Tractor 'Queen of Great Britain' (Works No.33486 - Reg. AD 8787) Built new for the War Office in 1919 and later sold to Coles Amusements when it was converted for showland use. It worked the West Country fairs until 1950 when it was laid up until purchased for preservation. Seen here in 1990, when owned by Jim & Joan Cook from Lea Cross, Shrewsbury.

Photo: David Bradbury

(left) Ruston & Hornsby (4hp compound) Tractor 'The Lincoln Imp' (Works No.52607 - Reg. HP 2201 - New 1918) Owned by Mr & Mrs A.J. Semple. *(right)* Aveling & Porter (4hp) Tractor 'Oberon' (Works No.11839 - Reg. SM 6448) owned by H.E. & B.E. Allison of Neston, Cheshire. Pictured here in 1990. A very fine pair of steam tractors both having been owned by Mr J.M. Crowther of Long Preston.

Photo: Malcolm Ranieri

This line up of Frank Lythgoe's fine collection of Showman's Engines in 1990, our last year at Bishop's Castle, probably sums up best the 21 years that we were there. From left to right, McLaren 'Goliath', Burrell Scenic 'Dolphin', Foden 'Prospector', Fowler 'King Carnival II' and Burrell 'Dreadnought'.

Photo: John Brooks

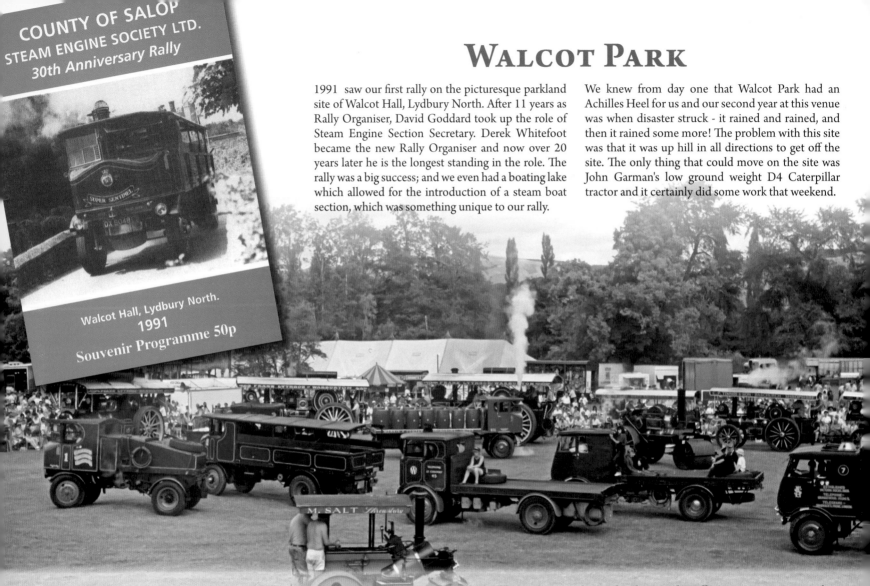

WALCOT PARK

1991 saw our first rally on the picturesque parkland site of Walcot Hall, Lydbury North. After 11 years as Rally Organiser, David Goddard took up the role of Steam Engine Section Secretary. Derek Whitefoot became the new Rally Organiser and now over 20 years later he is the longest standing in the role. The rally was a big success; and we even had a boating lake which allowed for the introduction of a steam boat section, which was something unique to our rally.

We knew from day one that Walcot Park had an Achilles Heel for us and our second year at this venue was when disaster struck - it rained and rained, and then it rained some more! The problem with this site was that it was up hill in all directions to get off the site. The only thing that could move on the site was John Garman's low ground weight D4 Caterpillar tractor and it certainly did some work that weekend.

COUNTY OF SALOP
STEAM ENGINE SOCIETY LTD.
30th Anniversary Rally

Walcot Hall, Lydbury North.
1991
Souvenir Programme 50p

If you've ever wondered what the Grand Parade looks like from the commentators' point of view, then here's a photo taken by David Bradbury, our commentator for over 45 years now, showing a very fine display of Sentinels in the arena at Walcot Park in 1991.

Photo: David Bradbury

Clayton & Shuttleworth roller (Works No.46688 - Reg. EP 3137) pictured here at the 1991 rally with Walcot Hall as a back drop. The roller had been to all of our rallies since 1962 but this was to be its penultimate year as the fire box was getting very long in the tooth. Owned at the time by Geoff Minshall of Chetton, Bridgnorth.

Photo: Malcolm Ranieri

Burrell Showman's (8hp) Road Locomotive 'Dreadnought' (Works No.3093 - Reg. AY 9682 - New 1909) First attended our 1974 rally, but when compared with that earlier photo in this book, the paintwork is seen to be much more conservative in this photo. In the background is an 89 key Marenghi fairground organ, which was new in 1909 to Arthur Holland of Swadlincote. Both the engine and organ, seen here in 1991, are owned by Frank Lythgoe of Lymm, Cheshire.

Photo: Malcolm Ranieri

Burrell SCC (8tons) Road Roller (Works No.2623 - Reg. MA 8207) New to S. Jackson & Sons of Wistaston, Crewe in 1903 and worked for them all its working life, but then stood derelict for many years. It returned to working order in 1990 and was purchased by the present owner Bob Bailey in 1990. Pictured here in 1991 at Walcot Park, one of its very few appearances on a rally field.

Photo: J B Toy

Gibbons & Robinson (7hp) Traction Engine (Works No.959 - Reg. AY 9874) New to a Mr Thomas Swain of Warrington in June 1891, this was last of only seven built and the only survivor. By 1929 it was owned by John Reed of Haywood, Hereford and last used in 1941 by Fred Williams of Preston-on-Wye, Hereford. Rescued in 1961 by Dick Phillips of Church Stretton then purchased in 1978 by R. Hesbrook of Upper Wellington, Hereford in a dismantled state and completely rebuilt, as seen here in 1991.

Photo: John Brooks

Fowler Traction Engine 'Pride of the Wye' (Works No.9225 - Reg. CF 3795) Purchased in 1963 by the present owner, Tom Henderson of Whitney-on-Wye, Herefordshire, who stripped it down and restored it. He rallied it until October 1987 when the engine was stripped down once again and a new firebox fitted. Seen here in 1991, which was also Tom's last year as our Chairman after six years in the role.

Photo: Malcolm Ranieri

Frank Lythgoe's fine collection of Showman's Engines often gave this demonstration of the power of the Steam Engine. Pictured here in 1991 we see the Fowler 'King Carnival II' towing the Burrell Scenic 'Dolphin', McLaren 'Goliath', Burrell 'Dreadnought' and finally the Foden 'Prospector' at the back, a load of approximately 100 tons.

Photo: David Bradbury

Stanley (10hp) Steam Car (Works No.7333 - Reg. DS 7696 - New 1913) Along with the move to Walcot Park in 1991, there was also the introduction of a new section for steam cars, although we had previously had one or two steam car entries as far back as 1965. The Stanley in this photo was rebuilt in Ireland after being imported from the USA and owned by W. Lowe of Beckenham, Kent.

Photo: J B Toy

Foden Traction Engine 'King George V' (Works No.2654 - Reg. E 6584 - New 1912) Seen here in 1991 when owned by G. Barlow of Lymm, Cheshire. Besides their distinctive cylinders, Foden's can be identified by their enormous rear wheels. This one was returned to Foden after a farm fire and subsequently worked for William Barlow of High Legh, Cheshire. It last worked in 1940 and took part in the great Centenary Parade at Foden's in 1956.

Photo: John Brooks

Sentinel S4 Waggon (Works No.9016 - Reg. HV 3865) New to E & A Shadrack of London in 1934 and worked for them up until the late 1940's. Purchased by E. Shone in the 1960's and then acquired by the present owner, B. Cousins of Daventry, Northants in 1987. Seen here at our 1992 rally when the rain just did not seem to stop!

Photo: Alan Johnson

Walcot Hall has a very fine boating lake in its parkland grounds and, we think, we were the first steam engine rally to ever have a Steam Launch section. The boats were even kept over night in the Hall's original boathouse. All of the boats seen in this picture were steam powered.

Photo: Malcolm Ranieri

21ft Steam Launch 'Pod's Puffin' seen here enjoying the calm waters of Walcot lake in 1991. Built by the owner at the time, Arthur Podmore, South Wirral and first steamed in 1985.

Photo: John Brooks

ONSLOW PARK

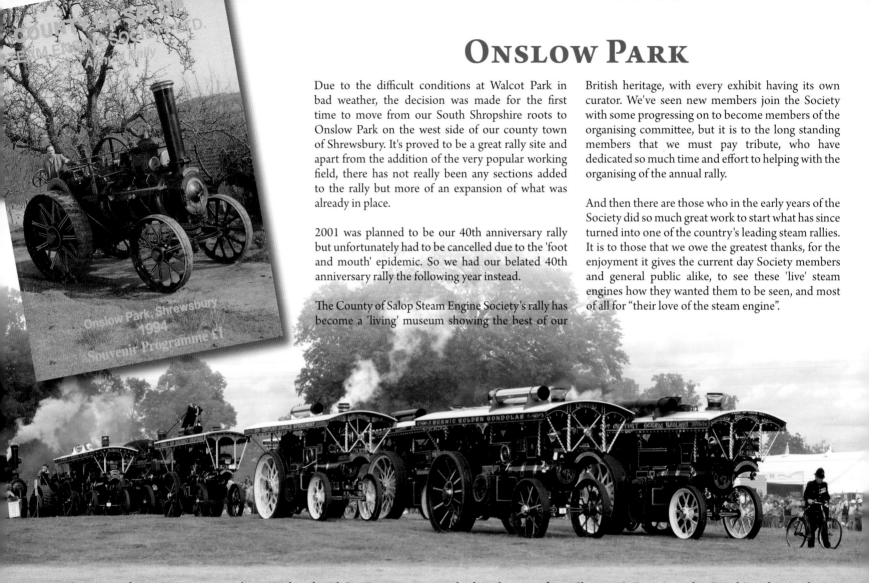

Due to the difficult conditions at Walcot Park in bad weather, the decision was made for the first time to move from our South Shropshire roots to Onslow Park on the west side of our county town of Shrewsbury. It's proved to be a great rally site and apart from the addition of the very popular working field, there has not really been any sections added to the rally but more of an expansion of what was already in place.

2001 was planned to be our 40th anniversary rally but unfortunately had to be cancelled due to the 'foot and mouth' epidemic. So we had our belated 40th anniversary rally the following year instead.

The County of Salop Steam Engine Society's rally has become a 'living' museum showing the best of our

British heritage, with every exhibit having its own curator. We've seen new members join the Society with some progressing on to become members of the organising committee, but it is to the long standing members that we must pay tribute, who have dedicated so much time and effort to helping with the organising of the annual rally.

And then there are those who in the early years of the Society did so much great work to start what has since turned into one of the country's leading steam rallies. It is to those that we owe the greatest thanks, for the enjoyment it gives the current day Society members and general public alike, to see these 'live' steam engines how they wanted them to be seen, and most of all for "their love of the steam engine".

In this picture from 2007, we see our long standing friend, Joe Davies once again leading the magnificent Showman's Engines in the Grand Parade, a tradition spanning the five decades that our society has now been holding annual steam rallies.

Photo: Steve Whitefoot

Aveling & Porter Roller 'Lady Hesketh' (Works No.9264 - Reg. EJ 966) This engine attended the first rally and the 21st anniversary. Seen here in 1991 owned by S & R Milns, Cockshutt, Ellesmere, Shropshire. Pictured again later in the book after a major overhaul.

Photo: Malcolm Ranieri

Fowler (8hp) Showman's Road Locomotive 'Renown' (Works No.15653 - Reg. CU 978) New to J. Murphy in 1920 to help work their Proud Peacocks Scenic Ride. Owned by Howard Brothers, Kirk Ireton, Derbyshire in this photo from 1994.

Photo: Malcolm Ranieri

A Horizontal Reciprocating Saw in the Working Arena in 1994. Recently recovered from Llangedwyn Mill in 1993 by Joe Lawley of Churchstoke, where it had been powered by a water wheel. Here it's being powered by the Burrell (7hp) Traction Engine (Works No.3794 - Reg. TA 2130 - New 1919) which Gordon Williams of Hay-on-wye purchased in 1981, still having the same paint as when it was used commercially. Price when new was £999.00, which was a great deal of money in 1919.

Photo: John Brooks

Foster (7hp) Showman's Road Locomotive 'Admiral Beatty' (Works No.14153 - Reg. BE 7221 - New 1916) Originally a road locomotive and then converted to a showman's road locomotive in 1920 by its makers, then sold to Thurstons (Amusement Caterers). Seen here in 1994 owned by Frank Lythgoe of Lymm, Cheshire.

Photo: Malcolm Ranieri

Fowler Road Locomotive 'Atlas' (Works No.17105 - Reg. VM 2110) New in 1928 to Norman E. Box for heavy haulage and possibly the most famous road loco in preservation with many photographs of it hauling a variety of heavy loads during its working days. Seen here in 1995, when owned by James Harvey-Bathurst of Ledbury. It had towed three trailers to the rally up the A49 from its base at Eastnor Castle and was presented by the well known Bolton Steeplejack, Fred Dibnah.

Photo: David Bradbury

Davey Paxman (6nhp) Traction Engine 'Little Audrey' (Works No.16849 - Reg. AF 3373) New from the Royal Show in 1911 to H.H. Truscott of St Austell, Cornwall and then sold to a Mr Tonkin of Treburrick, Cornwall in 1945 for £8, finishing its working life in the 1950's. Bought in 1970 and dismantled by R. Stock of Radwinter, Essex, but then sold to W. Day of Kent in 1979. Still in a dismantled state, it was bought by W. Dakin of Sandbach, Cheshire in 1983 and rebuilt over the next seven years.

Photo: David Bradbury

Marshall Steam Tractor 'Jinglin' Geordie' (Works No.68823 - Reg. BE 3044) New in 1915 to P & W Anderson Contractors, Glasgow and worked until 1937 before being bought for preservation in 1947 by the late Ian Fraser of Arbroath and was given to Leicester Museums in 1975. After extensive repairs, its only ever appearance at Onslow Park was in 2000 having travelled under its own steam from Coalville, Leicestershire.

Photo: Ian Cooper

Sentinel Loco (Works No.9535) New to the Coal Board at Silverdale Colliery. Based at the Foxfield Railway and owned in 2002 by Alan Williamson of Endon, Stoke-on-Trent.

Photo: Stephanie Semple

Sentinel S4 Waggon (Works No.8843 - Reg. UJ 2112) Started life as a three way tipper and delivered coal to the Sentinel Works with H.A.L. Price of Dawley. Later with H.V. Bowen of Welshpool and bought in 1977 as a derelict chassis with all the tipping gear missing. As can be seen in this photo from 2002, it was rebuilt as a timber tractor by Justin Gould's Father and is still owned by the Gould Family of Peasedown St. John, Bath.

Photo: Malcolm Ranieri

Burrell (8nhp) Showman's Road Locomotive 'The Masterpiece' (Works No.2072 - Reg. AD 8786) New in 1898 to John Cole of Bristol to haul and light his Savage Gallopers. Bernard Cole sold it in 1955 to Jim Hutchens of Ferndown and then it sold again in 1980 to Mr Martin Saunders of Ascot. It's the oldest Double Crank Compound Showman's Engine still in existence, seen here in 2002 when owned by Kelston Sparkes of Stanton Drew, Bristol, who purchased it in 1990 and restored it with his son Alan.

Photo: Malcolm Ranieri

Garrett Steam Tractor 'Princess Mary' (Works No.33278 - Reg. DP 4479) New in 1918 to the Ministry of Munitions, converted to Showman's Tractor, and also named at this time, for H. Wadbrook of Cardiff by Charles Openshaw of Reading, but later returned to its original tractor form. Seen here in 2002, owned by Mr Jonathan Garman of Leintwardine, Craven Arms.

Photo: Stephanie Semple

Fowler BB1 Ploughing Engine (Works No.15148 - Reg. CT 4663) Seen here in 2002 owned by Mr Michael Priestner of Dunham Massey, Altrincham, Cheshire.

Photo: Malcolm Ranieri

Joe Davies, a long standing friend of the Society and retired Police Officer, leading the Grand Parade in 2002, a job which he has done for many years and did so once again at our 50th Anniversary Rally in 2011. On the left is Burrell Scenic Showman's Road Locomotive 'Lord Lascelles' (Works No.3886 - Reg. XF 8162) and on the right is Burrell Showman's Road Locomotive 'Pride of Worcester' (Works No.2894 - Reg. FK 1463).

Photo: Stephanie Semple

Sentinel DG4 (Works No.8571) under the Sentinel Guard at the original Sentinel Works main gate in 2005 when some of the waggons, to mark the centenary of Sentinel moving to Shrewsbury in 1905, took part in a run starting at the original factory in Glasgow and finishing at the Sentinel Works on Whitchurch Road.

Photo: Malcolm Ranieri

The special line up in 2005 to mark the centenary of Sentinel moving to Shrewsbury, and arranged in order of age, which starting nearest the camera is Standard, Supers, DG and lastly the S types.

Photo: Malcolm Ranieri

Super Sentinel Timber Tractor 'The Elephant' (Works No.5644 - Reg. 757 CCT) Originally built to work in the Sentinel Works at Shrewsbury and worked on Teignmouth docks, Devon from 1931 until it retired at the same time as its driver, Tom Jones in 1963. It was rallied in this country in the early 1970's before being bought by Mr Hondema, Holland who kindly brought it over to help with the Centenary celebrations in 2005.

Photo: Malcolm Ranieri

Every year we try to have something different and in 2006 we had a display of unrestored engines. This imported hulk is an Aveling & Porter Road Locomotive (Works No.5192) owned by Anthony Seddon of Whitchurch, Shropshire. Behind is Aveling & Porter 10 ton Roller (Works No.8290 - Reg. E 5341) recently purchased in 2006 by Ian Cooper of Shrewsbury.

Photo: Malcolm Ranieri

Fowler K7 Ploughing Engine 'Linkey' (Works No.14257 - Reg. KE 2494) New in 1916 to Pickering & Higgins of Eastbridge, Kent and later worked up until 1948 for Link Bros of Newchurch. After standing idle until 1960 it had several owners until being purchased by the present owner in 1999. Seen here in 2007 owned by Mr Mark Jones of Droitwich, Worcester.

Photo: Brian Dobbs

Fowler Super Lion Crane Engine (Works No.17212 - Reg. RF 6092) New to John Thompson Boiler Engineers of Ettingshall, Wolverhampton in 1929 and used for delivering boilers until 1948, then used for general crane work around the firm's stockyard until 1958. Specially steamed in 1960 to pull the 10,000[th] boiler out of the works for delivery to Rolls Royce in Shrewsbury. Bought by Len Crane of Lanesfield, Wolverhampton in 1969 and regularly attends events all over the UK and Europe as seen here in 2007.

Photo: Brian Dobbs

Sentinel S4 Waggon (Works No.9293 - Reg. UJ 9497) A demonstrator for the Sentinel Works until being purchased by Castle Firebrick Co. of Northop, Flintshire in 1938. Purchased in 1956 and owned for a short time by our old friend Dick Woolley of Bucknell. Seen here in 2007 having recently been refurbished into period livery. Owned by Stuart Gray of Hitchin, Hertfordshire.

Photo: Brian Dobbs

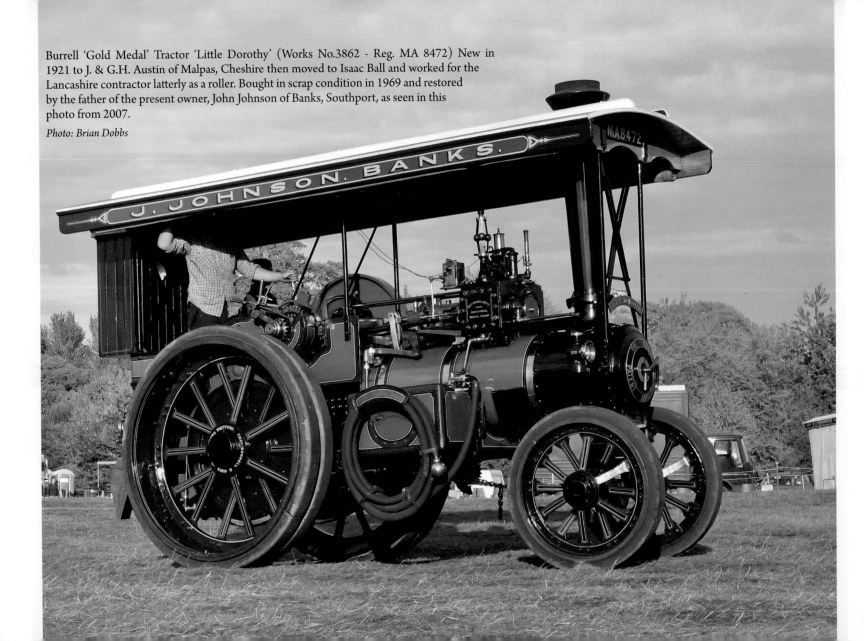

Burrell 'Gold Medal' Tractor 'Little Dorothy' (Works No.3862 - Reg. MA 8472) New in 1921 to J. & G.H. Austin of Malpas, Cheshire then moved to Isaac Ball and worked for the Lancashire contractor latterly as a roller. Bought in scrap condition in 1969 and restored by the father of the present owner, John Johnson of Banks, Southport, as seen in this photo from 2007.

Photo: Brian Dobbs

Aveling & Porter Traction Engine 'Valentine' (Works No.2436 - Reg. KE 6281) New in 1889 to Lorenzo Fuller of Dartford, Kent then sold at auction in 1924 to G.E. Gates. Used on a threshing round until 1948 before being purchased for preservation in 1959 by Mr Val Dunnett, a London artist. First steamed again in 1999 and bought in 2002 by the present owner Mr Neil Williams, Eglwys Cross, Whitchurch. Seen here in 2009.

Photo: Steve Whitefoot

(*Left*) Burrell Scenic Showman's Road Locomotive 'Lord Lascelles' (Works No.3886 - Reg. XF 8162) New in 1921 to Frederick Gray and then Harry Gray. In 1964 it was in the ownership of the legendry Steve Neville. Purchased by Mr C. Richard Marsh in 1981 who spent the next 12 years on an extensive rebuild. Purchased by Alan Williams of Holt, Wrexham in 2007.

(*Right*) Our local Showman's Engine, Burrell Showman's Road Locomotive 'Earl Haig' (Works No.3979 - Reg. YA 9138) New as a road locomotive in 1924 to W.J. Taylor of Midsomer Norton, Somerset and used for dredging operations. Converted to full showman's specification in 1934 for Mrs F. Symonds of Gloucester, working with travelling fairs throughout the West Country and London. Purchased by David Hilditch of Middletown, Welshpool in 2006.

Photo: Malcolm Ranieri

On the left, Burrell Showman's Road Locomotive 'Earl Haig', as above.

On the right, Burrell Scenic Showman's Road Locomotive 'General Gough' (Works No.3888 - Reg. NO 2379) New in 1921 to Swales Bolesworth of Dagenham. Passed to D.W. White of Margaretting, Essex and then bought by Jesse Vines of Hardwicke, Glos. Bought for preservation in 1952 by Viv Kirk of Oxford. Owners: Nigel & Beverley Myers & Sons, Rufforth, York.

Photo: Brian Dobbs

Burrell Scenic Showman's Road Locomotive 'Ex Mayor' (Works No.4000 - Reg. WT 8606) Worked all its life for G.T. Tuby of Doncaster. Built to a very special order, which was for it to be a narrow engine and have a long spring travel. So to achieve this it was built to a much older design than the other Burrell Scenics. Seen here in 2010, owned by J. & T. Saunders of Stotfold, Bedfordshire.

Photo: Malcolm Ranieri

Fowler Ploughing Engine 'The Chief' (Works No.2528 - Reg. AL 8834) New in 1875 to the Derbyshire Steam Cultivating Co, later with Beeby Bros of Rempstone, who continued steam cultivation through until the 1960's. It was dismantled in the 1920's and stored as spare parts, which were auctioned by Beeby Bros in 1988 and went through various hands to Guy Debes of Chapel-en-le-Frith in 2005, who rebuilt the engine, finally returning it to steam in May 2008 and seen here in 2010.

Photo: Brian Dobbs

Fowler Ploughing Engine 'Charlie' (Works No.15332 - Reg. AL 9854) Pictured in 2010 during its first year being rallied after major boiler work and overhaul. Owner: David Williams of Hay-on-Wye, Herefordshire.

Photo: Brian Dobbs

Sentinel Waggon (Works No.8122 - Reg. OF 5783) worked right up until 1982, making it the last commercially operated steam vehicle in the UK. Purchased in 2002 and completely restored by the present owner, David Hilditch of Middletown, Welshpool. Seen here in 2011, during a steam party held by the society in Church Stretton as part of our 50th Anniversary celebrations, in a re-enactment of the start of the 21st road run back in 1982.

Photo: Dave Parry

Showman's Road Locomotive 'Lord Nelson' (Works No.2879 - Reg. NO 698) Purchased new by Henry Thurston of Stanstead, Essex, then sold to F. Harris of Ashington, Sussex where she carried the name 'Sweet Nothing' as it was said that this was what it would pull on wet grass after being fitted with rubber tyres. It ended up in Hardwick's scrap yard in West Ewell until it was purchased for preservation in 1957 and eventually given the patriotic name of 'Princess Royal'. Purchased by the present owner in November 2009, who returned the engine to its original name of 'Lord Nelson'. The engine is at present in the care of Neil & John Boughey of Much Wenlock, Shropshire. John has been Treasurer and later Chairman of our Society. Owner: Peter Jones, Andreas, Isle of Man.. The engine is seen parked outside the Bucks Head, the location of the inaugural meeting called by our founder Mr Dennis Smith on the 7th June 1961.

Photo: Russell Davies

Burrell Agricultural Engine 'Spider' (Works No.3017 - Reg. KE 2739) Seen here passing through Little Stretton on its way to Church Stretton for the 50th Anniversary Steam Party. This engine spent its working life in Kent and Essex working for Wingham Agricultural Engineering. Owned by Alistair Evans of Bishop's Castle, Shropshire.

Photo: Malcolm Ranieri

Sentinel Standard Waggon (Works No.3976 - Reg. NY 344) New in 1921 to Crosswell's Brewery, Cardiff, until 1946 when it was purchased by J. Radcliffe, Forest of Dean. It lay derelict until 1962 when it was purchased by Dick Woolley and then by John Nudd of Telford in 1976 and rebuilt over a period of 4 years. Its current owner, Andrew Wheeler of Craven Arms, has carried out considerable work on this waggon since he purchased it, and is in a very appropriate period livery. Seen here in Burway Road after the Societies Steam Party in Church Stretton on Aug 14th 2011.

Photo: Steph Davies

Aveling & Porter (6ton) Steam Roller 'Ophelia' (Works No.8794 - Reg. FX 7043) Purchased in 1992 from a playground in Pontypridd and rebuilt over the next 12 years. Seen here going through Little Stretton to the 50th Anniversary Steam Party in 2011. Owned by Mr Brian Allison of Whixall, Whitchurch.

Photo: Malcolm Ranieri

Marshall Steam Tractor 'The Mascot' (Works No.68754 - Reg. CH 2462) New to Eastern Counties Haulage, Ipswich then later converted to a roller and sold in 1927 to Robert Bridson & Co. of Neston. Seen here in 2011 being steered by Ian Cooper and driven by Hedd Jones of Market Drayton, who's family have owned it since 1969. Making good speed, and smoke, heading towards Bishop's Castle from Horderley after the society steam party in Church Stretton.

Photo: Dianne Llewellyn

As a special event for our 50th Anniversary, it was decided to have a 26 mile road run from Bishop's Castle to Onslow Park, Shrewsbury. Here we see the Mayor of Bishop's Castle, Keith Pinches, assisted by our Chairman, John Onions about to start the first engine on its way by ringing the bell, which is being held by one of the younger enthusiasts, Alex Evans.

'The Bell', as it is only ever called, was first used by the Society in 1982 for our 21st Anniversary, to start the road run from Church Stretton to Bishop's Castle.

Although the origins of 'The Bell' are not exactly known, it is believed to be from a Continental railway locomotive.

Photo: Russell Davies

Burrell Convertible engine 'Old Duch' (Works No.2417 - Reg. AF 4393) owned by Ian Holt of Doncaster. Pictured here framed by a pair of showman's engines, early in the morning as the Evans shed is emptied of engines ready for the 50th Anniversary Road Run. The run started at the past site of the Bishop's Castle rallies, now Ransfords Saw Mill, along the A490 through Churchstoke, then the B4386 towards Shrewsbury and the ultimate destination at Onslow Park.

Photo: Russell Davies

Davey Paxman Agricultural Engine 'Little Audrey' (Works No.16849 - Reg. AF 3373) owned and driven by Will Dakin with David Hyde steering. One of the early departures from Bishop's Castle towing a regular attendee of the societies rallies, Marshall Portable (Works No.79936) owned by David Jones of Shrewsbury.

Photo: Russell Davies

By mid morning the later starters has risen and lit their engines, here in the field adjacent to the sawmill yard. Adrian Bailey is tending Aveling & Porter Showman's Tractor (Works No.6093 - Reg. D 2800), normally based in Cheshire.

Photo: Russell Davies

Foster Wellington Tractor 'Ikanopit' (Works No.14608 - Reg. PN 5629) owned by David Harding of Tamworth. Seen here some way into the run, cresting the long rise leaving Churchstoke, crewed by Chris Arrowsmith and Emily Hilditch. Earlier in the week, and in a single day, Chris had driven the engine from Fairford, Gloucestershire to attend the event, a distance of approximately 90 miles.

Photo: Steve Cornes

Aveling & Porter 'Betsy' (Works No.7632 - Reg. DM 3079) coming down the bank into Brockton. The engine was made famous by its late owner, Fred Dibnah of Bolton, and is now in the capable hands of his sons Jack and Roger.

Photo: Brian Dobbs

Sentinel Waggon (Works No.8122 - Reg. OF 5783) owned by David Hilditch of Middletown, Welshpool, in its last working owners livery, leads the way for another double geared Sentinel Waggon (Works No.8571 - Reg KF 6482) owned by the Goddard family of Shrewsbury.

Photo: Brian Dobbs

Aveling & Porter Convertible Roller 'Lady Hesketh' (Works No.9264 - Reg. EJ 966) Having just arrived at the lunch stop at Brockton, Steve and Doug Milns are looking for a parking space. Much midnight oil had been spent on this engine in the days preceding the event following a thorough overhaul. The huge effort was because the engine had also attended the inaugural 1961 rally and the 21st Anniversary Road Run.

Photo: Nick Bosworth

Engines from far and wide was the flavour of the engine park at the lunchtime stop in Brockton.

Photo: Nick Bosworth

Sentinel S4 (Shaft Drive) Waggon (Works No.8843 - Reg. UJ 2112) owned by Justin Gould of Bath. This waggon spent its entire working life locally in Shropshire and Montgomeryshire. Seen here outside The Cock Inn at Brockton, the road run's lunchtime venue.

Photo: Brian Dobbs

Burrell Showman's Road Locomotive 'Perseverance the Second' (Works No.3483 - Reg. WR 9110) then owned by the late James Gilbey of Compton Pauncefoot, Somerset. Parked adjacent to the brook in Brockton while its crew enjoys lunch.

Photo: Steve Cornes

Marshall (5 ton) Tractor 'The Mascot' (Works No.68754 - Reg. CH 2462) owned by Hedd Jones of Market Drayton, seen here going through Worthen. The Marshall had earlier in the year been driven from its base, near Woore, to Much Marcle in Herefordshire as well as to Bishop's Castle, via the earlier society anniversary event at Church Stretton, in order to participate in the road run.

Photo: Brian Dobbs

Fowler Road Loco 'Cynorthwywr' (Works No.15787 - Reg. EP 2398) owned by Richard and Phil Jeffs of Streetly, but based at Klondyke Mill at Draycott in the Clay. Seen here at Worthen, this was another engine driven to the event from its base via events at Bridgnorth and the earlier society event at Church Stretton.

Photo: Brian Dobbs

Fowler Ploughing Engine 'Margaret' (Works No.1368 - Reg. AL 8468) Andy Melrose and his engine, originally built in 1870, came all the way from Somerset to take part. He and his team gallantly put up with the backward 'tank' steering and iron shod wheels for the whole 26 miles!

Photo: Nick Bosworth

Ruston, Proctor & Co Tractor 'The Lincoln Imp' (Works No.52607 - Reg. HP 2201) Seen here, complete with Ruston traction wagon, approaching the summit of Nox Bank. This engine has been locally based for many years in the ownership of the Semple Family.

Photo: Brian Dobbs

Fowler haulage & winding engine (Works No.14950 - Reg. VF 2984) owned by David Williams of Hay-on-Wye, seen here climbing Nox Bank with only a few miles left before reaching Onslow Park.

Photo: Brian Dobbs

Garrett Tractor (Works No.33278 - Reg. DP 4479) owned by John Garman. As usual the engine is crewed by Matthew Daw and Chris Reeves, who run the engine from their base in Warwickshire and are seen here also nearing the summit of Nox Bank.

Photo: Brian Dobbs

McLaren General Purpose Engine (Works No.127 - Reg. HO 5618) was another Klondyke Mill based engine that travelled by road to the event. Steve Arrowsmith is seen here cutting across from Nox towards Ford on his son Chris's engine.

Photo: Brian Dobbs

Garrett Tractor 'Lord Raglan' (Works No.33738 - Reg. BJ 4791) nicely presented towing a period tipping trailer. This engine had been with Joe Powell at Ashton Keynes in Wiltshire for many years. Now owned by Richard and Tony Waistell of Binfield, Bracknell, Berkshire.

Photo: Brian Dobbs

Fowler T3 roller (Works No.17071 - Reg. BF 4887) and Eddison van. Allison and Graham Morrison, seen here coming down the bank into Brockton for the lunch stop, actually did the road run route in both directions, starting at their base near Sandbach, Cheshire.

Photo: Brian Dobbs

Aveling & Porter (6 ton) Roller 'Ophelia' (Works No.8794 - Reg. FX 7043) Brian Allison of Whixall and his crew brought the family's ex Eddison (Brecon) Machine, which ended its days at the Ynysangharad Park in Pontypridd as a piece of children's playground equipment.

Photo: Brian Dobbs

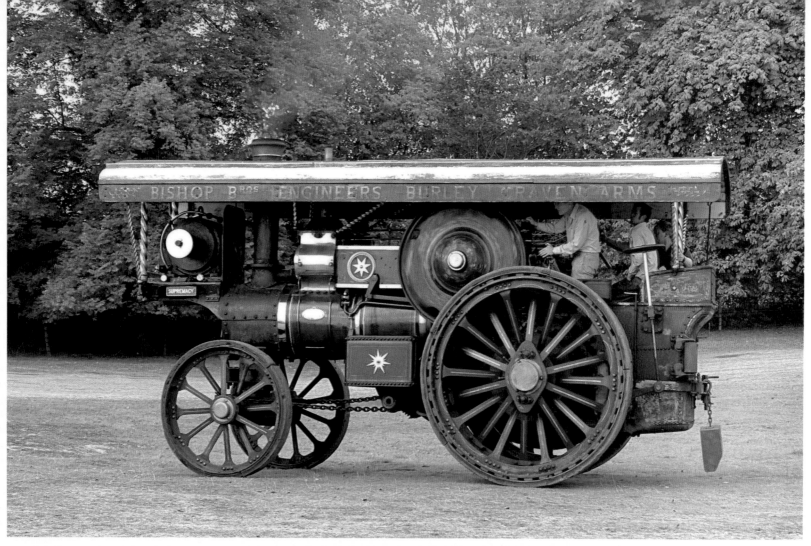

Fowler Showman's Road Locomotive 'Supremacy'. The 2011 50th Anniversary Rally begins and pictured here is, without a doubt, the star of the show after a gap of almost 40 years. Much effort had been put in by a few people to make this incredible moment possible. Looking as splendid as ever, apart from the faded paintwork, our flagship engine made a triumphant return to our rally, and with 'Bishop Bros Engineers Craven Arms' still visible on the canopy side boards.

Photo: Peter Donovan

The post horn gallop begins and bang on 2pm the two lead engines slowly move forward, just as they have done for 50 years. However, this time it was better than ever with it being the 50th Anniversary and our flagship 'Supremacy' was back! And even on the right hand side, just as it had been in the very first parade as had been immortalised in a photo by Barry J. Finch back in 1961, and seen on the Foreword page of this book. And he also returned in 2011 to see it again - we thank you Barry.

Photo: Brian Dobbs

Burrell Showman's Road Locomotive 'Endurance' (Works No.2547 - Reg. BL 8368) New to J.K. Cooper & Sons of Maidenhead, Berkshire as a road locomotive but converted, and named, for showland use for Maurice Stokes of Basingstoke, Hants. A first time visitor to our event after a 15 year rebuild by its present owner, Len Crane of Wolverhampton.

Photo: Steve Cornes

Ransomes Agricultural Engine 'Jesse' (Works No.27524 - Reg. E 5123) owned by the Jones Family, Forest of Dean. On the right is Aveling & Porter Convertible Roller 'Lady Hesketh' (Works No.9264 - Reg. EJ 966) owned by Steve Milns, Ellesmere - just back in steam after a major rebuild, having received a new boiler barrel, throat and tube plates, a motion overhaul, a new canopy and total re-paint. Both engines attended the 1961 rally when in the ownership of Vin Nash of Plealey.

Photo: Steve Cornes

Ransomes, Sims & Jefferies Traction Engine (Works No.15609 - CJ 4220) Owned by Geoff Lee's during our early rallies and came back, under its previous name of 'Salopian' from that time, for our 50th Anniversary Rally. Usually named 'Lady Diana' and now owned by the Prout Family of Ledbury, Herefordshire.

Photo: Steve Cornes

Fowler Agricultural Engine 'Tommy' (Works No.15710 - Reg. MO 780) New to Mr Dennis Sharpe of Stanford-in-the-Vale, Oxfordshire (was in Berkshire) where it spent most of its life threshing and baling. It was purchased in 1953 for preservation by Arthur Napper of Appleford, who is considered by many to be the founder of the modern traction engine rally movement. Owned in 2011 by Ray Matthews of Much Wenlock, Shropshire.

Photo: Dianne Llewellyn

(left) Foden D Type Timber Tractor (Works No.14084 - Reg. AMB 300) New in 1933 to James Murch of Umberleigh, Devon and used for threshing and timber haulage. Then sold to Jesse Vines followed by Cliff James of Kingswinford, who in 1951 gave it to Eric Middleton of Hartlebury, near Kidderminster. Purchased by Ian Sparks in 1985 in a very derelict condition and recently purchased by its present owner, David Walker of Mentmore, Bucks. *(right)* Foden D Type Timber Tractor 'Shropshire Lad' (Works No.13784 - Reg. UX 9728) Re-tubed just in time for the 2011 rally and owned by Bob Bailey of Horsehay, Telford.

Photo: Steve Cornes

Allchin Agricultural Engine 'Rebel' (Works No.1546 - Reg. AP 9079) First attended one of our rallies at Walcot Park in 1993. Owned by Allen Eaton of Creaton, Northamptonshire.

Photo: Dianne Llewellyn

(left) Foden 5 Ton Wagon 'Irene' (Works No.4258 - Reg. M 5798 - New 1914) Presented as a steam bus as Fodens used to carry workers to the Foden Works. Owned by Mr Alan Painter of Scholar Green, Stoke on Trent. *(right)* Foden 5/6 Ton Wagon Model HH 'Lady Catherine' (Works No.13848 - Reg. RB 3525) New to Derbyshire CC as a 3 way tipper to work in the council quarries and later bought by Dick Woolley of Bucknell. Owned by Peter Jones of Andreas, Isle of Man.

Photo: Brian Dobbs

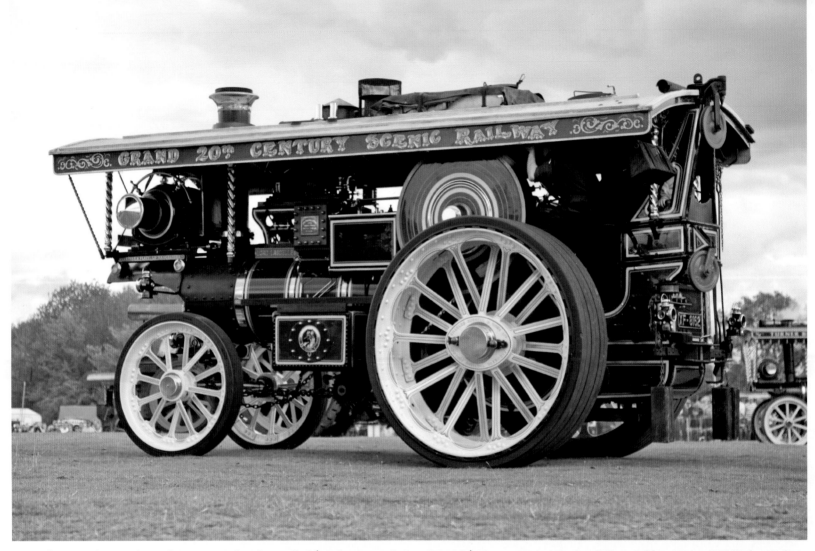

Burrell Scenic Showman's Road Locomotive 'Lord Lascelles' (Works No.3886 - Reg. XF 8162) New in 1921 to Frederick Gray. Sold in 1951 to J.W. Hickey & Son then in 1964 it was sold to the legendry Steve Neville. Richard Marsh purchased the engine in 1981 and spent the next 12 years on an extensive rebuild. Purchased in 2007 by the present owner, Alan Williams of Holt, Wrexham.

Photo: Philip Davies

Foster Agricultural Engine 'Winnie' (Works No.12539 - Reg. MA 5730) Another of our very old friends which came to our 2nd rally in 1962 with the late Jim Dakin and changed hands in 1976 to join the Frank Lythgoe Collection. Presented by Phil Moston of Holmes Chapel, Cheshire.

Photo: Dianne Llewellyn

Burrell Gold Medal Tractor 'Harry' (Works No.3442 - Reg. AH 0119) New in 1913 to S.M. Price of Llowes, Radnorshire but delivered to and initially based at Craven Arms, Shropshire where it was used for timber haulage. It remained in the Price Family until 1986, when it was sold at auction to L.J. Searle, the late grandfather of the current owner, Sarah Marsh of Horsham, West Sussex.

Photo: Peter Donovan

(nearest the camera) Foden D Type Tractor (Works No.13784 - Reg. UX 9728) New in 1931 to John Ashworth & Co of Newport, Shropshire. Owned by Bob Bailey of Horsehay, Telford. *(2nd from camera)* Foden HH 5/6 Ton Wagon (Works No.13624 - Reg. WX 2682) Owned by Gareth Jones of Dorking, Surrey. *(3rd from camera)* Foden 5 Ton Tipping Wagon (Works No.6216 - Reg. M 8562) Built in 1916 for the War Department. Owned by M.J. Wilkinson of Blackpool. *(4th from camera)* Foden C Type 6 Ton Wagon (Works No.11850 - Reg. MB 9404) New in 1925 to W.J. King of Bishops Lydeard. Owned by Russell Cook of Bridgnorth, Shropshire.

Photo: Brian Dobbs

Aveling & Porter Steam Tractor 'Dougal' (Works No.6021 - Reg. D 2608) Purchased in 1906 for the Rickmansworth & Uxbridge Valley Water Co. Preserved initially by D. Charlett in Oxford. Owned by Roddy Swain of Whitchurch. At the rear is Marshall Agricultural Engine 'Challenger' (Works No.57304 - Reg. TM 4430) Supplied new via Thurlows of Stowmarket to G. Lucas of Shinfield, Berkshire and used for threshing and haulage work. Purchased in March 2008 by Stuart Phillips of Newport, Shropshire.

Photo: Brian Dobbs

Wallis & Steevens Steam Roller 'Pepperpot' (Works No.7936 - Reg. OT 5187) originally purchased by Chaplow & Sons of Kendal in 1927, who were, and still are, road contractors. It was later purchased in a dilapidated state by Colonel R.E.C. Jennings of Kidwelly. First rallied at Bishop's Castle in 1973 and has since been to most of our society's rallies, under the ownership of Mike Salt of Wem, Shropshire.

Photo: Stoomwalsenclub Nederlands

Sentinel S4 Flat Waggon (Works No.9003 - Reg. VE 9963) seen on the left here, it worked for Paul Bros, flour millers in Cambridge and then Seacombe, Cheshire. Purchased in 1978 by the present owner, Peter Wareing of Preston and took part in the John O'Groats to Lands End run in 1999. On the right is Sentinel S4 Waggon (Works No.8884 - Reg. TJ 3319) bought straight from work by the present owner, Mr Alan Williamson of Endon, Stoke-on-Trent, rebuilt and rallied since the 1960's.

Photo: Brian Dobbs

Mann Patent Steam Cart & Wagon Co Steam Tractor 'Myfanwy' (Works No.1325 - Reg. U 4748) New onto Anglesey and spent all its working life there. 2011 was its first season back in steam after a very thorough overhaul by its owners, John and Mary Phillips of Rhoscolyn, Anglesey.

Photo: Peter Donovan

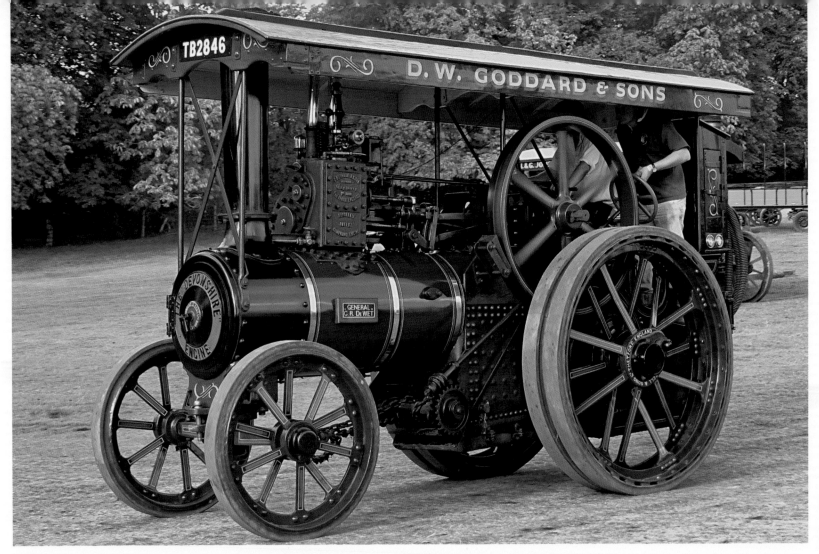

Burrell Devonshire Traction Engine 'General C.R. De Wet' (Works No.2512 - Reg. TB 2846 - New 1902) Purchased by the present owner in 1964 and has been to 18 of our rallies, the first visit being back in 1972, as pictured back in the Bishop's Castle section of the book. Owned by the Goddard Family of Montford Bridge, Shrewsbury.

Photo: Peter Donovan

Sentinel DG4 Waggon (Works No.8571 - Reg. KF 6482) Purchased new in 1931 by Samuel Banner & Co. Ltd of Bootle, Liverpool and later owned by Paul Bros Ltd of Seacombe, Cheshire. Seen at early traction engine rallies, when it was one of seven Sentinels owned by Edgar Shone of Cricklewood, London. Purchased by David Goddard of Montford Bridge, Shrewsbury in 1977 and painted in the Morris's colours as on their Sentinels operated 80 years ago.

Photo: Steve Whitefoot

Stanley Steam Car (30hp) Model 85 (Reg. DS 8662) Imported in 1990 from Nashville, Tennessee, USA by the present owner, David Goddard of Montford Bridge, Shrewsbury. Toured extensively in both the USA and UK, and has been to most of our rallies since. David is a long standing member of the Society in which time he has been Rally Organiser, Steam Engine Section Secretary and is currently Steam Car Section Secretary.

Photo: Philip Davies

Stanley Steam Car (9hp) Model E2 (Reg. SV 7389 - New 1909) Purchased by the present owner, Mrs Diana Goddard of Montford Bridge, Shrewsbury in 1998 from Paul Bourdon of Vermont, USA who had owned it since the mid 1940's. It was damaged in a barn fire in Massachusetts in 1976 and had a new boiler fitted in 1998. Diana, like her husband, David, has also been a long standing member of the Society and used to be our Secretary.

Photo: Peter Donovan

Stanley Steam Car (20hp) Model 'R' Type (Reg. SV 8635 - New 1909) completely rebuilt by the previous owner. Now owned by David Webster, who has also previously owned a Fowler Roller 'Evening Star', a Sentinel S4 and a Sentinel S6. He is a long standing member of the Society and was our Ring Master for many years.

Photo: Peter Donovan

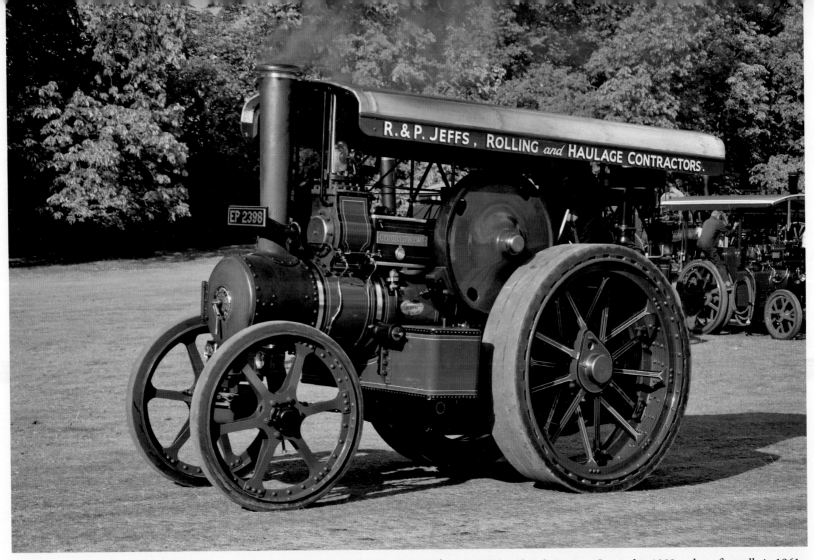

Fowler D5 3 Speed Road Locomotive 'Cynorthwywr' (Works No.15787 - Reg. EP 2398) Attended the Church Stretton Carnival in 1959 and our first rally in 1961 (*see picture and more history near front of book*) Acquired by the current owner, Philip Jeffs of Sutton Coldfield, 8 years ago and totally restored. What a pity Dick Tanner did not live to see his beloved engine steam again.

Photo: Steve Cornes

(Left) Sentinel S6 Tipper (Works No.8821 - Reg. BRF 200) Sold new to Tarmac and worked through the war years until 1946. Restored in the early 1970's by Richard Parkinson of Exeter, then onto David Webster and came to many of our rallies. Owned by Peter Walker & Diane Carney of Ackenthwaite, Cumbria, since being purchased in 1996.

(Right) Sentinel S8 (Works No.9105 - Reg. UJ 3652) The only single drive S8 constructed and was Sentinels own demonstrator. Acquired by Edgar Shone in the 1970's in scrap condition from Robert Wynn & Sons in South Wales, and has been to many of our rallies. Owned by Richard Hazell of Reading and in the care of Dave Roberts of Wickford, Essex.

Photo: Steve Cornes

Tasker Steam Tractor (4nhp) 'The Horses Friend' (Works No.1296 - Reg. BY 160) New in 1902 to two old ladies in Crystal Palace who felt sorry for the cart horses working on the hill outside their house - so they purchased the engine to pull the loads up the hill for the horses, and so it was subsequently owned by the R.S.P.C.A. It has been owned by the Moores Family of Liverpool for many years now, but in the care of John Johnson of Banks, Southport. Seen here driven by Hedd Jones.

Photo: Steve Llewellyn

Aveling & Porter Steam Roller (Works No.7632 - Reg. DM 3079) Owned originally by Flintshire County Council during its working days and restored by the late Fred Dibnah. Now owned by his sons, Jack and Roger.

Photo: Steve Llewellyn

Burrell Showman's Road Locomotive 'Fermoy' (Works No.3090 - Reg. OH 5022) Seen at earlier years rallies in this book and nice to see it back at our rally in 2011. A very well known engine in South Shropshire and formally owned by W.A. Bishop & Sons of Burley, as well as Dick Woolley of Bucknell, and presently owned by Russell Cook of Bridgnorth.

Photo: Stoomwalsenclub Nederlands

Foster Traction Engine 'Sprig' (Works No.14410 - Reg. UP 6481) Seen here driving Joe Lawley's saw bench in the Working Field. New in 1920 to J. Gregory & Son, a threshing contractor in Co. Durham, then sold into Lincolnshire in the 1930's, where it worked until late the 1940's. Bought by John Bosworth of Derby in 1971, who has carried out major repairs.

Photo: Brian Dobbs

Fowler Traction Engine 'Pride of the Wye' (Works No.9225 - Reg. CF 3795) There has been over 350 different engines attend our rallies over the 50 years since 1961, and this engine has the highest attendance rate, with a total of 40 appearances. Owned by Tom Henderson, a former Chairman of the society, and seen here in the working area that Tom has organised for many years.

Photo: Stoomwalsenclub Nederlands

McLaren General Purpose Engine (Works No.127 - Reg. HO 5618) New in 1882 to F.G. Dalgety of Lockerley Hall, Romsey, Hampshire. Bought for preservation in 1963 by John Crawley, who rallied it until 1969 when it went to the late John Mayes. He then rallied it until the late 1980's when it was acquired by the present owner, Chris Arrowsmith, of Burton-on-Trent.

Photo: Steve Cornes

Burrell Agricultural Engine 'Diamond Queen' (Works No.2003 - Reg. YA 509) New to a farm in Dorset in 1897, the year of Queen Victoria's Diamond Jubilee. Rescued in the 1950's, from a scrap yard in Bristol by Richard Wilcox. Pictured earlier in the book when it attended our 1962 rally in Church Stretton. Owned by Peter Brown of Stroud, Gloucestershire.

Photo: Steve Whitefoot

Ruston & Hornsby Steam Tractor 'Princess Anne' (Works No.52766 - Reg. AW 4996) Bought for preservation for £75 by Bill Griffiths in 1957, attended the Church Stretton Carnival in 1959, our first rally in 1961 and is still owned by the same family. Owned by Rose Griffiths of Kidderminster.

Photo: Steve Cornes

Sentinel Super Tractor 'Maggie May' (Works No.5558 - Reg. PD 1854) New in 1924 to Hodgsons Brewery until 1930. Bought by Criddles in 1933 and used by them until 1963, the same year it first came to our rally in the ownership of Dennis Wedgwood of Stoke-on-Trent. Bought in 1965 by the present owners family. Owned by Tim Clarke of Macclesfield, Cheshire.

Photo: Stoomwalsenclub Nederlands

Marshall Tractor (Works No.65650 - Reg. BE 2227) Bought in 1958 for £45 by Jonathan Garman of Leintwardine, aged just 19 at the time. He acquired the surviving tractor parts from the local scrap yard and it attended the first Church Stretton rally in 1961 as a roller. It was rebuilt as a tractor by its new owner, Neil Thompson of Aberystwyth, but sadly its crankshaft broke at our 2011 rally so it was towed by Jonathan Garman's Garrett.

Photo: Steve Cornes

The Golden Film Shield

Generally considered to be the National Traction Engine Trust's premier trophy, which was given to the trust by Morris & Company, now known as Morris Lubricants, in 1958.

Norman Owen, our former Chairman, always insisted that each years rally must be better than the previous one, and fortunately each year he was indeed able to say "It's the best yet".

So Norman would have been very proud when the County of Salop Steam Engine Society was awarded this trophy in 2011 for not only putting on a fantastic 50th Anniversary Rally and Road Run, but for all the hard work that everyone involved has put in over those 50 years to make it the success that it is today.